Focus on Grammar

An **INTERMEDIATE** Course for Reference and Practice

VOLUME A

Focus on Grammar

An **INTERMEDIATE** Course for Reference and Practice

SECOND EDITION

Marjorie Fuchs

Margaret Bonner

Miriam Westheimer

To the memory of my parents, Edith and Joseph Fuchs—MF

To my parents, Marie and Joseph Maus, and to my son, Luke Frances—MB

To my husband, Joel Einleger, and my children, Ari and Leora—MW

FOCUS ON GRAMMAR: AN **INTERMEDIATE** COURSE FOR REFERENCE AND PRACTICE, **VOLUME A**

Pearson Education, 10 Bank Street, White Plains, NY 10606

Editorial director: Allen Ascher
Executive editor: Louisa Hellegers
Director of design and production: Rhea Banker
Development editor: Françoise Leffler
Production manager: Alana Zdinak
Managing editor: Linda Moser
Senior production editor: Virginia Bernard
Senior manufacturing manager: Patrice Fraccio
Manufacturing manager: David Dickey
Photo research: Beth Boyd
Cover design: Rhea Banker
Cover image: *Elm, Middleton Woods, Yorkshire,
    6 November 1980.* Copyright © Andy Goldsworthy
    from his book *A Collaboration with Nature*,
    Harry N. Abrams, 1990.
Text design: Charles Yuen
Text composition: Preface, Inc.
Illustrators: Moffitt Cecil: pp. 17, 18, 156, 208, 359, 388; Ronald
    Chironna: pp. 24, 33 (br), 34, 191, 215, 239, 250, 251, 296, (bm), 272;
    Brian Hughes: pp. 14, 244, 247 (tl, br), 272, 292; Jock MacRae: pp. 45, 94,
    181, 183, 302, 304, 314, 316; Paul McCusker: pp. 37, 41, 44, 103; Andy
    Myer: pp. 52, 149, 184, 205; Dusan Petricic: pp. 2, 7, 8, 15, 58, 86, 171,
    176, 193, 198, 247 (tr, bl), 404; PC&F: pp. 46, 51, 398, 407, 408, 409.
Text and photo credits: see p. xiv

Library of Congress Catalog-in-Publication Data

Fuchs, Marjorie,

    Focus on grammar, An intermediate course for reference and practice /
    Marjorie Fuchs, Margaret Bonner, Miriam Westheimer.—2nd ed.
        p. cm.
    ISBN 0-201-34681-8 (alk. paper)
    1. English language textbooks for foreign speakers. 2. English language—
Grammar problems, exercises, etc.   I. Bonner, Margaret, II. Westheimer, Miriam.
III. Title.

PE1128.F794 1999
428.2'4'076—dc21

                                                      99-23208
                                                      CIP

        6 7 8 9 10—CRK—04

CONTENTS

PART III

MODALS AND RELATED VERBS AND EXPRESSIONS

PART IV

PRESENT PERFECT

APPENDICES

ABOUT THE AUTHORS

Marjorie Fuchs has taught ESL at New York City Technical College and LaGuardia Community College of the City University of New York and EFL at the Sprach Studio Lingua Nova in Munich, Germany. She holds a Master's Degree in Applied English Linguistics and a Certificate in TESOL from the University of Wisconsin–Madison. She has authored or co-authored many widely used ESL textbooks, notably *On Your Way: Building Basic Skills in English, Crossroads, Top Twenty ESL Word Games: Beginning Vocabulary Development, Around the World: Pictures for Practice, Families: Ten Card Games for Language Learners, Focus on Grammar: A High-Intermediate Course for Reference and Practice*, and the workbooks to the *Longman Dictionary of American English*, the *Longman Photo Dictionary, The Oxford Picture Dictionary*, and the *Vistas* series.

Margaret Bonner has taught ESL at Hunter College and the Borough of Manhattan Community College of the City University of New York, at Taiwan National University in Taipei, and at Virginia Commonwealth University in Richmond. She holds a Master's Degree in Library Science from Columbia University, and she has done work towards a Ph.D. in English Literature at the Graduate Center of the City University of New York. She has contributed to a number of ESL and EFL projects, including *Making Connections, On Your Way*, and the Curriculum Renewal Project in Oman, where she wrote textbooks, workbooks, and teachers manuals for the national school system. She authored *Step into Writing: A Basic Writing Text*, and co-authored *Focus on Grammar: A High-Intermediate Course for Reference and Practice* and *The Oxford Picture Dictionary Intermediate Workbook*.

Miriam Westheimer taught EFL at all levels of instruction in Haifa, Israel, for a period of six years. She has also taught ESL at Queens College, at LaGuardia Community College, and in the American Language Program of Columbia University. She holds a Master's Degree in TESOL and a doctorate in Curriculum and Teaching from Teacher's College of Columbia University. She is the co-author of a communicative grammar program developed and widely used in Israel.

INTRODUCTION

THE **FOCUS ON GRAMMAR** SERIES

Focus on Grammar: An Intermediate Course for Reference and Practice, Second Edition, is part of the four-level *Focus on Grammar* series. Written by practicing ESL professionals, the series focuses on English grammar through lively listening, speaking, reading, and writing activities. Each of the four Student Books is accompanied by an Answer Key, a Workbook, an Audio Program (cassettes or CDs), a Teacher's Manual, and a CD–ROM. Each Student Book can stand alone as a complete text in itself, or it can be used as part of the series.

BOTH CONTROLLED AND COMMUNICATIVE PRACTICE

Research in applied linguistics suggests that students expect and need to learn the formal rules of a language. However, students need to practice new structures in a variety of contexts to help them internalize and master them. To this end, *Focus on Grammar* provides an abundance of both controlled and communicative exercises so that students can bridge the gap between knowing grammatical structures and using them. The many communicative activities in each unit enable students to personalize what they have learned in order to talk to each other with ease about hundreds of everyday issues.

A UNIQUE FOUR-STEP APPROACH

The series follows a unique four-step approach. In the first step, **grammar in context,** new structures are shown in the natural context of passages, articles, and dialogues. This is followed by a **grammar presentation** of structures in clear and accessible grammar charts, notes, and examples. The third step is **focused practice** of both form and meaning in numerous and varied controlled exercises. In the fourth step, **communication practice,** students use the new structures freely and creatively in motivating, open-ended activities.

A COMPLETE CLASSROOM TEXT AND REFERENCE GUIDE

A major goal in the development of *Focus on Grammar* has been to provide Student Books that serve not only as vehicles for classroom instruction but also as resources for reference and self-study. In each Student Book, the combination of grammar charts, grammar notes, and expansive appendices provides a complete and invaluable reference guide for the student.

THOROUGH RECYCLING

Underpinning the scope and sequence of the series as a whole is the belief that students need to use target structures many times in many contexts at increasing levels of difficulty. For this reason new grammar is constantly recycled so that students will feel thoroughly comfortable with it.

COMPREHENSIVE TESTING PROGRAM

SelfTests at the end of each part of the Student Book allow for continual assessment of progress. In addition, diagnostic and final tests in the Teacher's Manual provide a ready-made, ongoing evaluation component for each student.

THE **INTERMEDIATE** STUDENT BOOK

Focus on Grammar: An Intermediate Course for Reference and Practice, Second Edition, is divided into eight parts comprising thirty-eight units. Each part contains grammatically related units with each unit focusing on a specific grammatical structure. Where appropriate, contrast units present two contrasting forms (for example, the simple present tense and the present progressive). Each unit has a major theme relating the exercises to one another. All units have the same clear, easy-to-follow format:

GRAMMAR IN CONTEXT

Grammar in Context presents the grammar focus of the unit in a natural context. The texts, all of which are recorded, present language in various formats. These include newspaper and magazine excerpts, Web sites, e-mail messages, advertisements, instructions, questionnaires, and other formats that students encounter in their day-to-day lives. In addition to presenting grammar in context, this introductory section raises student motivation and provides an opportunity for incidental learning and lively classroom discussions. Topics are varied, including employment, the weather, marriage, homelessness, the environment, and future technology. Each text is preceded by a pre-reading activity called **Before You Read.** Pre-reading questions create interest, elicit students' knowledge about the topic, help point out features of the text, and lead students to make predictions about the reading.

GRAMMAR PRESENTATION

This section is made up of grammar charts, notes, and examples. The Grammar **charts** focus on the form of the unit's target structure. The clear and easy-to-understand boxes present each grammatical form in all its combinations. Affirmative and negative statements, *yes/no* and *wh-* questions, short answers, and contractions are presented for all tenses and modals covered. These charts provide students with a clear visual reference for each new structure.

The Grammar **notes** and **examples** that follow the charts focus on the meaning and use of the structure. Each note gives a clear explanation of the grammar point, and is always accompanied by one or more examples. Where appropriate, timelines help illustrate the meaning of verb tenses and their relationship to one another. *Be careful!* notes alert students to common ESL/EFL errors. Usage Notes provide guidelines for using and understanding different levels of formality and correctness. Pronunciation Notes are provided when appropriate. Reference Notes provide cross-references to related units and the Appendices.

FOCUSED PRACTICE

The exercises in this section provide practice for all uses of the structure presented in the Grammar Presentation. Each Focused Practice section begins with a "for recognition only" exercise called **Discover the Grammar.** Here, students are expected to recognize either the form of the structure or its meaning without having to produce any language. This activity raises awareness of the structures as it builds confidence.

Following the Discover the Grammar activity are exercises that practice the grammar in a controlled, but still contextualized, environment. The exercises proceed from simpler to more complex. There is a large variety of exercise types including fill-in-the-blanks, matching, multiple choice, question and sentence formation, and editing (error analysis). Exercises are cross-referenced to the appropriate grammar notes so that students can review the notes if necessary. As with the Grammar in Context, students are exposed to many different written formats, including letters, postcards, journal entries, resumes, charts, schedules, menus, and news articles. Many exercises are art-based, providing a rich and interesting context for meaningful practice. All Focused Practice exercises are suitable for self-study or homework. A complete **Answer Key** is provided in a separate booklet.

COMMUNICATION PRACTICE

The exercises in this section are intended for in-class use. The first exercise is **Listening.** After having had exposure to and practice with the grammar in its written form, students now have the opportunity to check their aural comprehension. Students hear a variety of listening formats, including conversations, radio announcements, weather forecasts, interviews, and phone recordings. After listening to the recording (or hearing the teacher read the tapescript, which can be found in the Teacher's Manual), students complete a task that focuses on either the form or the meaning of the structure. It is suggested that students be allowed to hear the text as many times as they wish to complete the task successfully.

The listening exercise is followed by a variety of activities that provide students with the opportunity to use the grammar in open-ended, interactive ways. Students work in pairs or small groups in interviews, surveys, opinion polls, information gaps, discussions, role plays, games, and problem-solving activities. The activities are fun and engaging and offer ample opportunity for self-expression and cross-cultural comparison. The final exercise in this section is always **Writing,** in which students practice using the structure in a variety of written formats.

REVIEW OR SELFTEST

After the last unit of each part, there is a review feature that can be used as a self-test. The exercises in this section test the form and use of the grammar content of the part. These tests include questions in the format of the Structure and Written Expression sections of the TOEFL®. An **Answer Key** is provided after each test, with cross-references to units for easy review.

FROM GRAMMAR TO WRITING

At the end of each part, there is a writing section called From Grammar to Writing in which students are guided to use the grammar structures in a piece of extended writing. Formats include a personal letter, a business letter, instructions, an informal note, and an essay. Students practice pre-writing strategies such as brainstorming, word-mapping, tree-diagramming, and outlining. Each writing section concludes with peer review and editing.

APPENDICES

The Appendices provide useful information, such as lists of common irregular verbs, common adjective-plus-preposition combinations, and spelling and pronunciation rules. The Appendices can help students do the unit exercises, act as a springboard for further classroom work, and serve as a reference source.

NEW IN THIS EDITION

In response to users' requests, this edition has:

- new and updated texts for Grammar in Context
- pre-reading questions
- a new easy-to-read format for grammar notes and examples
- cross-references that link exercises to corresponding grammar notes
- more photos and art
- more recorded exercises
- more information gap exercises
- more editing (error analysis) exercises
- a writing exercise in each unit
- a From Grammar to Writing section at the end of each part

SUPPLEMENTARY **COMPONENTS**

All supplementary components of *Focus on Grammar, Second Edition,* —the Audio Program (cassettes or CDs), the Workbook, and the Teacher's Manual—are tightly keyed to the Student Book. Along with the CD-ROM, these components provide a wealth of practice and an opportunity to tailor the series to the needs of each individual classroom.

AUDIO PROGRAM

All of the Listening exercises as well as the Grammar in Context passages and other appropriate exercises are recorded on cassettes and CDs. The symbol ▭ appears next to these activities. The scripts appear in the Teacher's Manual and may be used as an alternative way of presenting these activities.

WORKBOOK

The Workbook accompanying *Focus on Grammar: An Intermediate Course for Reference and Practice, Second Edition,* provides a wealth of additional exercises appropriate for self-study of the target grammar of each unit in the Student Book. Most of the exercises are fully contextualized. Themes of the Workbook exercises are typically a continuation or a spin-off of the corresponding Student Book unit themes. There are also eight tests, one for each of the eight Student Book parts. These tests have questions in the format of the Structure and Written Expression section of the TOEFL®. Besides reviewing the material in the Student Book, these questions provide invaluable practice to those who are interested in taking this widely administered test.

TEACHER'S MANUAL

The Teacher's Manual, divided into five parts, contains a variety of suggestions and information to enrich the material in the Student Book. The first part gives general suggestions for each section of a typical unit. The next part offers practical teaching suggestions and cultural information to accompany specific material in each unit. The Teacher's Manual also provides ready-to-use diagnostic and final tests for each of the eight parts of the Student Book. In addition, a complete script of the Listening exercises is provided, as is an answer key for the diagnostic and final tests.

CD-ROM

The *Focus on Grammar* CD-ROM provides individualized practice with immediate feedback. Fully contextualized and interactive, the activities broaden and extend practice of the grammatical structures in the reading, listening, and writing skill areas. The CD-ROM includes grammar review, review tests, and all relevant reference material from the Student Book. It can also be used alongside the *Longman Interactive American Dictionary* CD-ROM.

CREDITS

TEXT

Grateful acknowledgment is given to the following publishing companies and individuals for permission to print, reprint, or adapt materials for which they own copyrights:

The Warrior Workout. Adapted from "Body Jolt" by Laurie Tarkin. Published in *Fitness Magazine*, July/August 1998. Copyright © 1998 by Laurie Tarkin. Used by permission of Laurie Tarkin. **"This Used to Be My Playground,"** by Madonna Ciccone and Shep Pettibone © 1992 WB Music Corp., Webo Girl Publishing, Inc., MCA Music Publishing, a Division of MCA Inc. and Shepsongs Inc. All Rights o/b/o Webo Girl Publishing, Inc. administered by WB Music Corp. All Rights o/b/o Shepsongs, Inc. administered by MCA Music Publishing, a Division of MCA Inc. All Rights Reserved. Used by Permission.

PHOTOGRAPHS

Grateful acknowledgment is given to the following for providing photographs:

p. 11 *(left)* Eyewire, Inc.; **p. 11** *(center, right)* MEDIAFOCUS International, LLC; **p. 12** Stephen Danelian/ Exposure New York; **p. 19** Corbis/Asian Art & Archeology, Inc.; **p. 24** Corbis; **p. 26** Copyright © 1994 by Barbara Seyda. Reprinted by permission of Susan Bergholz Literary Services, New York; **pp. 27, 29** RubberBall Productions; **p. 30** Corbis/Bettmann; **p. 35** *(left)* Seth Poppel Yearbook Archives; **p. 35** *(right)* Corbis/Jim Lake; **p. 36** PhotoDisc Inc.; **p. 58** Corbis/Jennie Woodcock; **p. 65** Reflections Photolibrary; **p. 95** Cornell University Photography, photo by Frank DiMeo; **p. 99** Courtesy of Dr. Eloy Rodriguez; **p. 100** Courtesy of Corel and IWEC (International Wildlife Education & Conservation; **p. 114** Courtesy of Professional Flair and Mary Verdi Fletcher; **p. 118** Courtesy of Professional Flair and Mary Verdi Fletcher; **p. 142** Comstock; **p. 150** *(left)* HI-AYH Photo by Joe Hochner; **p. 150** *(right)* Swedish YHA; **p. 156** Courtesy of Hong Kong Youth Hostel Association; **p. 166** Corbis/S. Carmona; **p. 201** Courtesy of Robert Stolarick; **p. 208** PhotoDisc Inc.; **p. 213** PhotoDisc Inc.; **p. 216** *(left)* Corbis/Yogi, Inc.; **p. 216** *(right)* PhotoDisc Inc.; **pp. 226, 231, 234** Courtesy of Beth Boyd; **p. 235** Corbis/Bob Krist; **p. 254** AP/Wide World Photos; **p. 259** Corbis/Kevin R. Morris; **p. 260** AP/Wide World Photos; **p. 277** Centers for Disease Control and Prevention; **p. 281** *(1–7)* PhotoDisc Inc.; **p. 281** *(8)* RubberBall Productions; **p. 285** RubberBall Productions; **p. 291** Courtesy of PNI; **p. 298** RubberBall Productions; **p. 306** Copyright The New Yorker Collection, 1995, Robert Mankoff from cartoonbank.com; **pp. 312, 332** Courtesy of PNI; **p. 340** Courtesy of the New York State Governor's Traffic Safety Committee; **p. 344** Courtesy of Ben Leonard; **p. 350** Courtesy of Beth Boyd and Marjorie Fuchs; **p. 352** Spencer Grant/Photo Researchers, Inc.; **p. 358** Corbis/Ric Ergenbright; **p. 365** PhotoDisc Inc.; **p. 378** Copyright R. Calentine/Visuals Unlimited, Inc.; **p. 388** Corbis/Bettmann; **p. 394** PhotoDisc Inc.

ACKNOWLEDGMENTS

Before acknowledging the many people who have contributed to the second edition of *Focus on Grammar: An Intermediate Course for Reference and Practice*, we wish to express our gratitude to those who worked on the FIRST EDITION, and whose influence is still present in the new work.

Our continuing thanks to:

- **Joanne Dresner,** who initiated the project and helped conceptualize the general approach of *Focus on Grammar.*

- **Nancy Perry, Penny Laporte, Louisa Hellegers,** and **Joan Saslow,** our editors, for helping to bring the first edition to fruition.

- **Sharon Hilles,** our grammar consultant, for her insight and advice.

Writing a SECOND EDITION has given us the wonderful opportunity to update the book and implement valuable feedback from teachers who have been using *Focus on Grammar.*

We wish, first of all, to acknowledge the following consultants and reviewers for reading the manuscript and offering many useful suggestions:

- CONSULTANTS: **Marcia Edwards Hijaab**, Henrico County Schools, Richmond, Virginia; **Kevin McClure**, ELS Language Center, San Francisco; **Tim Rees**, Transworld Schools, Boston; **Alison Rice**, Director of the International English Language Institute, Hunter College, New York; **Ellen Shaw**, University of Nevada, Las Vegas.

- REVIEWERS: **Lynn Alfred**, William Rainey Harper College, Palatine, Illinois; **Sandra Banke**, Clark College, ESL, Vancouver, Washington; **Judy Cleek**, University of Tennessee-Martin; **Julie Cloninger**, English Language Program, Virginia Commonwealth University; **Mary Coiner**, J. Sargeant Reynolds Community College, Richmond, Virginia; **Diane De Echeandia**, Delhi Technical College, Delhi, New York; **Meg Flynn**, Avila College, Intensive Language and Culture Program, Kansas City, Missouri; **Irene Frankel**, Assistant Director of New School University, English Language Studies, New York; **Andrea Whitmore**, Applied Language Institute at Penn Valley Community College, Kansas City, Missouri.

(continued on next page)

We are also grateful to the following editors and colleagues:

- **Françoise Leffler**, editor *extraordinaire*, for her dedication, her keen ear, and her sense of style. We also appreciate her unstinting attention to detail and her humor, which had us looking forward to her calls. The book is undoubtedly better for her efforts.

- **Louisa Hellegers**, for being accessible and responsive to individual authors while coordinating the many complex aspects of this project.

- **Virginia Bernard**, for piloting the book through its many stages of production.

- **Irene Schoenberg**, author of the Basic level of *Focus on Grammar*, for generously sharing her experience in teaching our first edition and for her enthusiastic support.

- **Dr. Eloy Rodriguez**, for contributing his time and expertise as we developed the content for Unit 10. Much of the art in that unit is based on photographs from his fieldwork.

- **Andréa Cook, Gretchen Flint, Sharon Goldstein, Ian Harvey, Molly Heron, Vicky Julian, Lee Kurchinski, Phyllis Neumann, Thomas Saunders Pyle, Miriam Shakter**, and **Mark Smith**, for sharing with us their native-speaker intuition.

Finally, we are grateful, as always, to **Rick Smith** and **Luke Frances**, for their helpful input and for standing by and supporting us as we navigated our way through another *FOG*.

M.F. and M.B.

THE STORY BEHIND THE COVER

The photograph on the cover is the work of **Andy Goldsworthy**, an innovative artist who works exclusively with natural materials to create unique outdoor sculpture, which he then photographs. Each Goldsworthy sculpture communicates the artist's own "sympathetic contact with nature" by intertwining forms and shapes structured by natural events with his own creative perspective. Goldsworthy's intention is not to "make his mark on the landscape, but to create a new perception and an evergrowing understanding of the land."

So, too, *Focus on Grammar* takes grammar found in its most natural context and expertly reveals its hidden structure and meaning. It is our hope that students using the series will also develop a new perception and an "evergrowing" understanding of the world of grammar.

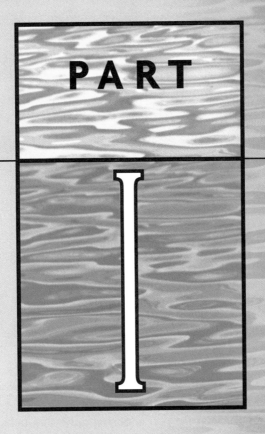

PART

I

PRESENT, PAST, AND FUTURE:
REVIEW AND EXPANSION

PRESENT PROGRESSIVE AND SIMPLE PRESENT TENSE

GRAMMAR **IN CONTEXT**

BEFORE YOU READ Look at the cartoons. What are the people doing? How do they feel?

 Read this article about cross-cultural communication.

WHAT'S YOUR CROSS-CULTURAL IQ?

Are you **living** in your native country or in another country? **Do** you ever **travel** abroad? **Do** you **understand** the misunderstandings below?
(Explanations appear at the bottom of the page.)

SITUATION 1   **SITUATION 2**

EXPLANATIONS

SITUATION 1:

Eva invited Karl to a seven o'clock party.

Karl **is arriving** at exactly 7:00 P.M. That**'s** polite in his culture.

In Eva's culture, people usually **arrive** at least a half an hour later than the scheduled time. That**'s** polite in her culture.

SITUATION 2:

Sami and Taro **are having** a conversation. They **are** both **feeling** uncomfortable.

In Sami's culture, people usually **stand** quite close to each other.

In Taro's culture, people **like** to stand farther apart, and they almost never **touch**.

GRAMMAR **PRESENTATION**

PRESENT PROGRESSIVE

SIMPLE PRESENT TENSE

AFFIRMATIVE STATEMENTS

SUBJECT	BE	BASE FORM OF VERB + -ING	
I	am*		
You	are		
He She It	is	traveling	now.
We You They	are		

AFFIRMATIVE STATEMENTS

SUBJECT		VERB	
I You		travel.	
He She It	often	travels.	
We You They		travel.	

*For contractions of *I am, you are,* etc., see Appendix 20, page A-8.

NEGATIVE STATEMENTS

SUBJECT	BE	NOT + BASE FORM OF VERB + -ING	
He	is	not traveling	now.

NEGATIVE STATEMENTS

SUBJECT	DO NOT / DOES NOT + BASE FORM OF VERB	
He	does not travel	often.

YES / NO QUESTIONS

BE	SUBJECT	BASE FORM OF VERB + -ING	
Is	he	traveling	now?

YES / NO QUESTIONS

DO / DOES	SUBJECT	BASE FORM OF VERB	
Does	he	travel	often?

SHORT ANSWERS

Yes,	he	is.
No,		isn't.

SHORT ANSWERS

Yes,	he	does.
No,		doesn't.

WH- QUESTIONS

WH- WORD	BE	SUBJECT	BASE FORM OF VERB + -ING	
Where	are	you	traveling	now?

WH- QUESTIONS

WH- WORD	DO / DOES	SUBJECT		BASE FORM OF VERB
Where	do	you	usually	travel?

| **NOTES** | **EXAMPLES** |

1. Use the **present progressive** (also called the present continuous) to describe something that is happening <u>right now</u>.

Now
|
She's speaking English.
Past————————X————————Future
|

- Eva **is talking** to Karl.
- At the moment, she**'s wearing** a robe.
- She**'s speaking** English right now.

Use the **simple present tense** to describe what <u>regularly</u> happens, what <u>usually</u> happens, or what <u>always</u> happens.

Now
|
Past—X—X—X—X—X—X—X—X—X— Future
She speaks | Spanish.

- Eva **talks** to Karl every day.
- She usually **wears** jeans.
- She **speaks** Spanish at home.

REFERENCE NOTE
For **spelling rules** on forming the **present progressive,** see Appendix 15 on page A-6.
For **spelling rules** on forming the third person singular of the **simple present** tense, see Appendix 16 on page A-6.
For **pronunciation rules** for the **simple present** tense, see Appendix 22 on page A-10.

---

2. Use the **present progressive** to describe something that is happening in the <u>extended present time</u> (for example, *nowadays, this month, these days, this year*), even if it's not happening at the moment of speaking.

Now
|
Past————————X————————Future
⌣
| She's studying.

- We**'re studying** U.S. customs *this month*.
- Laura**'s studying** in France *this year*.
- **Are** you **studying** hard *these days*?

Use the **simple present tense** with <u>adverbs of frequency</u> to express how often something happens.

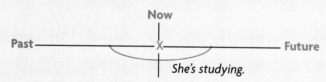

always   usually   often   sometimes   rarely / seldom   never
/ . . . . . / . . . . . / . . . . . / . . . . . /
100%   0%

- In Spain, women *always* **kiss** on both cheeks.
- In France, women *often* **kiss** on both cheeks.
- We *rarely* **stand** very close to each other.
- In China, children *never* **call** adults by their first name.

▶ **BE CAREFUL!** Adverbs of frequency usually come before the main verb, but they go after the verb *be*.

- They *never* **come** late.
- They **are** *never* late.

3. The **present progressive** is often used to show that the action is <u>temporary</u>.

- **I'm staying** with friends, but I plan to leave soon.

4. REMEMBER! **Non-action verbs** (also called stative verbs) usually <u>describe states or situations</u> but not actions. Most non-action verbs are <u>not</u> usually <u>used in the present progressive</u> even when they describe a situation that exists at the moment of speaking.

Non-action verbs:

a. express **emotions**
(*hate, like, love, want, feel*)

USAGE NOTE: Unlike other verbs that express emotion, *feel* is often used in the progressive form.

b. describe **mental states**
(*know, remember, believe, think [= believe], suppose, understand*)

c. show **possession**
(*have, own, possess, belong*)

d. describe **perceptions** and **senses**
(*hear, see, smell, taste, feel, notice, seem, look [= seem], be, appear, sound*)

▶ **BE CAREFUL!** Some verbs that describe perceptions and senses such as *taste, smell, feel,* and *look* can have both a non-action and an action meaning.

(See Appendix 2, page A-2, for a list of non-action verbs.)

- Jane **wants** to go home right now.
  NOT ~~Jane is wanting to go home now.~~

- I'm hungry. **I want** a hamburger.
  NOT ~~I'm wanting a hamburger.~~
- Ricki **feels** homesick.
  OR
- Ricki **is feeling** homesick.

- **I know** a lot of U.S. customs now.
- Ari **remembers** your number.

- Cesar **has** two brothers.
- Some students **own** cars.

- **I hear** the telephone.
- Dina **seems** tired.

- The soup **tastes** good. Try some.
- She**'s tasting** the soup to see if it needs more salt.

5. Use the **simple present tense** to talk about situations that are <u>not connected to time</u>—for example, scientific facts and physical laws.

- Stress **causes** high blood pressure.
- Water **boils** at 212° F=100° C.

REFERENCE NOTE
You can also use the present progressive and the simple present to talk about the **future**.
(See Unit 6.)

FOCUSED PRACTICE

1 DISCOVER THE GRAMMAR

*Read these journal entries by Brian, a Canadian summer exchange student studying in Argentina. Circle all the verbs that describe what is happening **now**. Underline the verbs that describe what **generally** happens.*

June 28: I'm sitting in a seat 30,000 feet above the earth en route to Argentina! I usually have dinner at this time, but right now I have a headache from the excitement. My seatmate is eating my food. She looks happy.

June 30: It's 7:30. My host parents are still working. Carlos, my father, works at home. My little brother Ricardo is cute. He looks (and acts) a lot like Bobby. Right now, he's looking over my shoulder and trying to read my journal.

July 4: The weather is cold here. I usually spend the first weekend of July at the beach. Today I'm walking around in a heavy sweater.

August 6: I feel so tired tonight. Everyone else feels great in the evening because they take long naps in the afternoon.

2 SCHEDULE CHANGES

Grammar Note 1

Look at Brian's schedule. Complete the sentences below. Use the present progressive or the simple present tense. Choose between affirmative and negative forms.

8:30–12:30	~~Attend class~~	Go on field trip to the Museum of the City
2:00–3:00	Eat lunch	
3:00–5:00	~~Take a nap~~	Work on my Web page
5:00–6:30	~~Do homework~~	(Call home at 5:00 sharp today!)
6:30–8:30	~~Play tennis~~	Watch a video with Eva
9:00	Have dinner	

1. Brian usually _____attends class_____ between 8:30 and 12:30, but today he

___is going on a field trip to the Museum of the City.___

2. He always _____ between 2:00 and 3:00.

3. He normally _____ after lunch, but today he _____

_____

4. It's 5:00, but he _____ homework now. He _____

_____ instead.

5. It's 6:20. He _____

6. It's 6:45, but he _____ tennis. He _____

_____ with Eva.

7. It's 9:00. Brian _____

3 DIFFERENT MEANINGS

Complete these conversations that take place outside of a classroom. Choose between the present progressive and the simple present tense of the verbs in parentheses.

1. **LI-WU:** Hi, Paulo. What _____ are _____ you _____ doing _____?
a. (do)

PAULO: Oh, I _____ for class to begin.
b. (wait)

LI-WU: How are you? You _____ tired.
c. (look)

PAULO: I am a little. I _____ evenings this semester. Hey, is that your
d. (work)

teacher over there?

LI-WU: Yes. She _____ to one of my
e. (talk)

classmates.

PAULO: I wonder what's wrong. He _____ at
f. (not look)

her. He _____ uncomfortable.
g. (look)

LI-WU: Oh. That _____ anything. In Taiwan
h. (not mean)

it's not respectful to look directly at your teacher.

2. **MORIKO:** Look, there's Miguel. He _____ to Luisa.
a. (talk)

NINA: Yes. They _____ a class together
b. (take)

this semester.

MORIKO: They _____ very close to each other.
c. (stand)

_____ you _____ they
d. (think)

_____?
e. (date)

(continued on next page)

NINA: No. I _____ it _____ anything special.
　　　　　　　　　f. (not think)　　　　　g. (mean)

I _____ from Costa Rica, and people normally _____
　　h. (come)　　　　　　　　　　　　　　　　　　　　　　i. (stand)

that close to each other.

3. **RASHA:** There's Hans. Why _____ he

_____ so fast? Class
　a. (walk)

_____ at 9:00. He still
　b. (start)

_____ ten minutes!
　c. (have)

CLAUDE: He always _____ fast. I think
　　　　　　　　　　　d. (walk)

people from Switzerland often _____ to be in a hurry.
　　　　　　　　　　　　　　　　　　e. (appear)

4. **YOKO:** Isn't that Sergio and Luis? Why _____ they _____
　　　　　　　　　　　　　　　　　　　　　　　　　　　　　a. (shake)

hands? They already _____ each other!
　　　　　　　　　　b. (know)

LI-JING: In Brazil, men _____ hands every
　　　　　　　　　　　　　c. (shake)

time they _____.
　　　　　　　d. (meet)

YOKO: _____ women _____
　　　　　　　　　　　　　　　　　　e. (shake)

hands too?

LI-JING: I really _____.
　　　　　　　　　　f. (not know)

---

④ CULTURE SHOCK!   Grammar Notes 1–4

Complete this paragraph. Use the correct form of the verbs in the box.

cause	feel	live	m~~a~~ke	travel

New food, new customs, new routines—they all _____*make*_____ international travel
　　　　　　　　　　　　　　　　　　　　　　　　　1.

interesting. But they also _____ culture shock in many travelers.
　　　　　　　　　　　　　2.

_____ you now _____ or _____ in a culture
　　　　　　　　　　　　3.　　　　　　　　4.

different from your own? If so, why _____ you _____ so good
　　　　　　　　　　　　　　　　　　　　　　　　　5.

(or so bad)? Take the quiz on the next page and learn more about the four stages of

culture shock.

Complete the following statements, using the correct form of the verbs in the box.
Then, check the statements that are true for you now.

annoy	feel	improve	love	make	treat	understand	want

a. I _____ it here!   ☐
   6.

b. People always _____ me very kindly.   ☐
   7.

c. The customs here often _____ me.   ☐
   8.

d. I _____ to go home!   ☐
   9.

e. My language skills _____ a lot this month.   ☐
   10.

f. I _____ a lot of new friends these days.   ☐
   11.

g. I still _____ everything, but I _____ at home.   ☐
   12. (negative)   13.

QUIZ RESULTS:
If you checked . . .   *You may be in the . . .*
a and **b**   **Honeymoon Stage:** In the first weeks everything seems great.
c and **d**   **Rejection Stage:** You have negative feelings about the new culture.
e and **f**   **Adjustment Stage:** Things are getting better these days.
g   **Adaptation Stage:** You are finally comfortable in the new culture.

5 EDITING

Read this student's journal. Find and correct eleven mistakes in the use of the
present progressive or simple present tense. The first mistake is already corrected.

○	It's 12:30 and I ~~sit~~ 'm sitting in the library right now. My classmates are eating lunch together, but I'm not hungry yet. At home, we eat never this early. Today our journal topic is culture shock. It's a good topic for me right now because I'm being pretty homesick. I miss my old routine. At home we always are eating a big meal at 2:00 in the afternoon. Then we rest. But here in Toronto I'm having a 3:00 conversation class. Every day, I almost fall asleep in class, and my teacher ask me, "Are you bored?" Of course I'm not bored. I just need my afternoon nap! This class always is fun. This semester, we work on a project with video cameras. My team is filming groups of people from different cultures. We are analyze "social distance." That means how close to each other these people stand. According to my new watch, it's 12:55, so I leave now for my 1:00 class. Teachers here really aren't liking tardiness!

COMMUNICATION PRACTICE

6 LISTENING

A school newspaper is interviewing a new foreign student. Listen. Then listen again and check the things the student usually does and the things she is doing now or these days.

	Usually	Now or These Days
1. speak English	☐	☑
2. speak Spanish	☐	☐
3. live in a small town	☐	☐
4. live in a big city	☐	☐
5. walk slowly	☐	☐
6. wear a watch	☐	☐
7. study computer sciences	☐	☐

7 GETTING TO KNOW YOU

Walk around your classroom. Ask your classmates questions. Find someone who . . .

	Name(s)
likes visiting foreign countries	_____
isn't wearing a watch	_____
speaks more than two languages	_____
is studying something besides English	_____
doesn't watch sports on TV	_____
is planning to travel this year	_____
_____ *(add your own)*	_____

EXAMPLE:
A: Do you like visiting foreign countries?
B: Yes, I do. What about you?

Report back to the class.

EXAMPLE:
Tania and José like visiting foreign countries.

8 WHAT'S HAPPENING?

Work in pairs. Look at the photographs. Describe them. What's happening?
Discuss possible explanations for each situation. Compare your answers to those
of your classmates.

EXAMPLE:

A: He's pointing. He looks angry.

B: Maybe he's just explaining something.

9 QUESTIONABLE QUESTIONS?

Work in small groups. Look at these questions. In your culture, which questions
are appropriate to ask someone you just met? Which are not appropriate?
Compare your choices with those of your classmates. Discuss appropriate and
inappropriate questions in an English-speaking culture you know.

Where do you come from?

How old are you?

What do you do?

How much rent do you pay?

What are you studying?

Are you married?

Do you have any children?

Where do you live?

Are you living alone?

How much do you weigh?

Why do you have only one child?

Are you wearing perfume?

10 WRITING

Write a paragraph about a new experience you are having. Maybe you are living
in a new country, taking a new class, or working at a new job. Describe the
situation. How is it different from what you usually do? How do you feel in
the situation?

EXAMPLE:

I usually live at home with my parents, but this month I'm living
with my aunt and uncle. Everything seems different. My aunt . . .

IMPERATIVE

GRAMMAR **IN CONTEXT**

BEFORE YOU READ Look at the pictures. What is the woman doing? What do *you* do to stay fit?

 *Read part of an exercise routine presented in a fitness magazine.*

THE WARRIOR WORKOUT

Having a bad day? **Don't let** it get you down. **Try** our kickboxing workout instead. You'll feel better *and* build your strength. **Do** it three times a week for fast results.

THE JAB
Get into the basic position: **Bend** your knees and **place** your right foot in front. **Raise** your fists with your right hand in front. Now **punch** with your right fist. **Don't stand** straight as you punch. Instead, **lean** forward for more power. **Bring** your fist back immediately. Then **change** sides.

THE POWER KICK
Get into the basic position and **move** your weight onto your right foot. **Bring** your left knee as high as your hip. Then **kick** to the side. **Point** your toes as you kick.

GRAMMAR **PRESENTATION**

IMPERATIVE

AFFIRMATIVE	
BASE FORM OF VERB	
Bend	your knees.
Raise	your fists.

NEGATIVE		
DON'T	**BASE FORM OF VERB**	
Don't	**stand**	straight.
	kick	to the front.

NOTES

1. Use the imperative to:

   a. give **directions** and **instructions**.

   b. give **orders** or **commands**.

   c. make **requests** (use *please* in addition to the imperative).

   d. give **advice** or make **suggestions**.

   e. give **warnings**.

   f. extend an **informal invitation**.

   ▶ **BE CAREFUL!** Do not use the imperative in formal situations (for example, when inviting a boss or a teacher).

EXAMPLES

- **Get** into the basic position.
- **Turn** left at the light.

- **Get up!**
- **Don't move!**

- *Please* **read** this article.
- **Read** this article, *please*.

- Always **warm up** first.
- **Don't exercise** when you're sick.

- **Be** careful!
- **Don't trip**!

- **Work out** with us tomorrow.
- **Bring** a friend.

- Would you like to join us, Mrs. Rivera?
  NOT ~~Join us, Mrs. Rivera.~~

---

2. Note that the <u>subject</u> of an imperative statement is *you*. However, *you* is <u>not said or written</u>.

▶ **BE CAREFUL!** The imperative form is the same in both the singular and the plural.

- **Stand up** straight.
- **Don't hold** your breath.

- John, **point** your toes.
- John and Susan, **point** your toes.

FOCUSED PRACTICE

❶ DISCOVER THE GRAMMAR

Match the imperative in column A with a situation in column B.

Column A

___g___ **1.** Don't touch that!

_____ **2.** Look both ways.

_____ **3.** Dress warmly!

_____ **4.** Don't bend your knees.

_____ **5.** Mark each answer true or false.

_____ **6.** Come in. Make yourself at home.

_____ **7.** Try a little more pepper.

Column B

a. Someone is visiting a friend.

b. Someone is going out into the cold.

c. Someone is crossing a street.

d. Someone is taking an exam.

e. Someone is exercising.

f. Someone is tasting some food.

g. Something is hot.

❷ HEALTH SHAKE   Grammar Notes 1a and 2

Match a verb from column A with a phrase from column B to give instructions for making a banana-strawberry smoothie. Then put the sentences in order under the correct pictures.

Column A

Add

Slice

Wash

Cut

Blend

Pour

Column B

the ingredients until smooth.

six strawberries.

a banana.

orange juice into the blender.

the strawberries in half.

the fruit to the orange juice.

1. _____Slice a banana._____

2. _____

3. _____

4. _____

5. _____

6. _____

3 **MARTIAL ARTS**

*Complete the advertisement for a martial arts school. Use the affirmative or
negative imperative form of the verbs in the box.*

become	choose	decrease	increase	learn
miss	register	take	~~think~~	wait

MARTIAL ARTS ACADEMY

_____Don't think_____ that martial arts is only about physical training. A good
　　　　a.

martial arts program offers many other benefits as well. _____
　　　　　　　　　　　　　　　　　　　　　　　　　　　　　　　　b.

self-defense and more at the Martial Arts Academy:

◆ _____ stress. Martial arts training helps you relax.
　　　c.

◆ _____ concentration. Martial arts students focus better.
　　　d.

◆ _____ fit. Strength and flexibility improve as you learn.
　　　e.

We are offering an introductory trial membership. _____ this special
　　　　　　　　　　　　　　　　　　　　　　　　　　　f.

opportunity. _____ classes with Master Lorenzo Gibbons,
　　　　　　　g.

a ninth-level Black Belt Master. _____ classes
　　　　　　　　　　　　　　　　h.

from our convenient schedule. _____!
　　　　　　　　　　　　　　i.

_____ now for a two-week trial.
　　j.

ONLY $20. ◆ UNIFORM INCLUDED.

4 **EDITING**

*Read this martial arts student's essay. Find and correct five mistakes in the use of
the imperative. The first mistake is already corrected.*

　　　　　　　　　　　　　　　　　　　　　　　　　　　　　　　　Write
For the Black Belt essay, Master Gibbons gave us this assignment: ~~You write~~
about something important to you. My topic is *The Right Way,* the rules of
life for the martial arts. First, respects other people—treat them the way
you want them to treat you. Second, helped people in need. In other words,
use your strength for others, not to use it just for your own good. Third,
no lie or steal. You can't defend others when you feel guilty. There are
many rules, but these are the most important ones to me.

COMMUNICATION PRACTICE

5 LISTENING

A TV chef is describing how to make pancakes. Listen. Then listen again and number the instructions in the correct order.

_____ Heat a frying pan and melt a small piece of butter in it.

__1__ Beat two egg whites in a large bowl.

_____ Add one and a quarter cups of whole wheat flour to the egg whites.

_____ Flip the pancakes over.

_____ Blend in some fruit.

_____ Mix thoroughly.

_____ Top them with fruit or yogurt.

_____ Pour some of the pancake mixture into the frying pan.

_____ Add a cup of low-fat milk.

6 RECIPE EXCHANGE

Work in groups. Write down one of your favorite recipes. List the ingredients and write the directions. Read it to your group. Answer any questions they have.

EXAMPLE:

QUICK AND EASY BEAN TACOS	
Ingredients:	1 can of beans (black, kidney, or pinto), 4 hard corn taco shells, 1 tomato, 1 onion, lettuce, salsa, spices (cumin, chili powder)
Directions:	Rinse and drain the beans. Add the spices. Simmer for 10 minutes. Chop the tomato and onion. Shred the lettuce. Fill the taco shells with the beans, tomatoes, and onion. Top with the lettuce and salsa.

A: How long do you rinse the beans?

B: Until the water looks clear. Use cold water. Don't use hot water.

7 CALM DOWN!

Work in small groups. Imagine you have been in a traffic jam for an hour. Someone is waiting to meet you on a street corner. What can you say to yourself to calm yourself down? Share your list with the other groups.

EXAMPLE:

A: Take a deep breath.

B: Don't think about the traffic.

C: . . .

8 INFORMATION GAP: FIND THE WAY

Work in pairs (A and B). You are both going to give driving directions to places on the map. Student B, turn to page 18 and follow the instructions there. Student A, trace the route from Carter and Adams to the Sunrise Gym. Be careful! One-way streets are marked → or ←. Don't go the wrong way on one-way streets! Give your partner directions. Ask your partner for directions to the Martial Arts Academy. Trace the route. Use sentences like these:

Start at Carter and Adams.	Go straight.	Continue on 9th Street.
(Don't) turn right.	Make a left turn.	Stay on Founders.

EXAMPLE:

> **A:** I want to go to the Martial Arts Academy. Can you give me directions?
>
> **B:** Sure. Start at Carter and Adams.

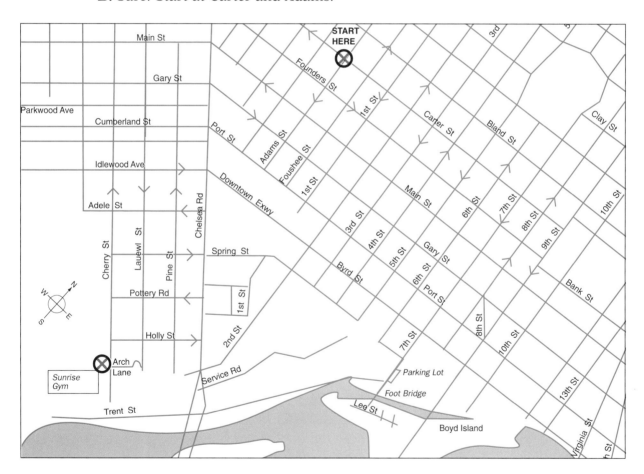

When you are finished, compare routes. Are they the same?

9 WRITING

Write directions from your school to another location. It can be your home, a store, the train station, or any place you choose.

Student B, trace the route from Carter and Adams to the Martial Arts Academy.
Give your partner directions. Ask your partner for directions to the Sunrise Gym.
Trace the route. Be careful! One-way streets are marked → or ←. Don't go the
wrong way on one-way streets! Use sentences like these:

Start at Carter and Adams.	**Go straight.**	**Continue on 9th Street.**
(Don't) turn right.	**Make a left turn.**	**Stay on Founders.**

EXAMPLE:

A: I want to go to the Martial Arts Academy. Can you give me directions?

B: Sure. Start at Carter and Adams.

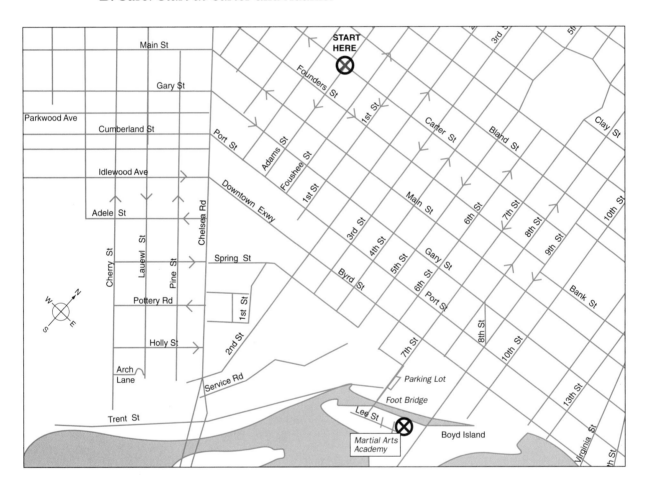

When you are finished, compare routes. Are they the same?

SIMPLE PAST TENSE

GRAMMAR **IN CONTEXT**

BEFORE YOU READ Look at the picture and the text next to it. What did Matsuo Basho do? How long did he live?

Read this excerpt from a biography of Japanese poet Matsuo Basho.

The old pond;
the frog.
Plop!

As for that flower
By the road—
My horse ate it!

First day of spring—
I keep thinking about
the end of autumn.

Matsuo Basho, 1644–1694

Matsuo Basho **wrote** more than 1,000 three-line poems called "haiku." He **chose** topics from nature, daily life, and human emotions. He **became** one of Japan's most famous poets, and his work **established** haiku as an important art form.

Matsuo Basho **was born** near Kyoto in 1644. He **did not want** to become a samurai (warrior) like his father. Instead, he **moved** to Edo (present-day Tokyo) and **studied** poetry. By 1681, he **had** many students and admirers.

Basho, however, **was** restless. Starting in 1684, he **traveled** on foot and on horseback all over Japan. Sometimes his friends **joined** him and they **wrote** poetry together. Travel **was** difficult in the seventeenth century, and Basho often **got** sick. He **died** in 1694, during a journey to Osaka. At that time he **had** 2,000 students.

GRAMMAR **PRESENTATION**

SIMPLE PAST TENSE: *BE*

AFFIRMATIVE STATEMENTS

SUBJECT	BE	
I	**was**	
You	**were**	
He She It	**was**	famous.
We You They	**were**	

NEGATIVE STATEMENTS

SUBJECT	BE NOT	
I	**wasn't**	
You	**weren't**	
He She It	**wasn't**	famous.
We You They	**weren't**	

YES / NO QUESTIONS

BE	SUBJECT	
Was	I	
Were	you	
Was	he she it	famous?
Were	we you they	

SHORT ANSWERS

	AFFIRMATIVE	
	you	**were.**
	I	**was.**
Yes,	he she it	**was.**
	you we they	**were.**

SHORT ANSWERS

	NEGATIVE	
	you	**weren't.**
	I	**wasn't.**
No,	he she it	**wasn't.**
	you we they	**weren't.**

WH- QUESTIONS

WH- WORD	BE	SUBJECT	
Where When Why	**was**	I	
	were	you	
	was	he she it	famous?
	were	we you they	

SIMPLE PAST TENSE: REGULAR AND IRREGULAR VERBS

AFFIRMATIVE STATEMENTS

SUBJECT	VERB	
I You He She It We You They	**moved** **traveled**	to Japan.
	came* **left***	in 1684.

NEGATIVE STATEMENTS

SUBJECT	*DID NOT*	BASE FORM OF VERB	
I You He She It We You They	**didn't**	**move** **travel**	to Japan.
		come **leave**	in 1684.

Come (came) and *leave (left)* are irregular verbs.
See Appendix 1 on page A-1 for a list of irregular verbs.

YES / NO QUESTIONS

DID	SUBJECT	BASE FORM OF VERB	
Did	I you he she it we you they	**move** **travel**	to Japan?
		come **leave**	in 1684?

SHORT ANSWERS

	AFFIRMATIVE	
Yes,	you I he she it you we they	**did**.

SHORT ANSWERS

	NEGATIVE	
No,	you I he she it you we they	**didn't**.

WH- QUESTIONS

WH- WORD	*DID*	SUBJECT	BASE FORM OF VERB	
When Why	**did**	I you he she it we you they	**move** **travel**	to Japan?
			come? **leave**?	

NOTES	EXAMPLES

1. Use the **simple past tense** to talk about actions, states, or situations that are now **finished**.

Now

Past ————X———————————————— Future
He was a poet.

- Basho **lived** in the seventeenth century.
- He **was** a poet.
- He **wrote** *haiku*.
- He **didn't stay** in one place.
- Where **did** he **travel**?

---

2. You can use the simple past tense with **time expressions** that refer to the past. Some examples of past time expressions are *last week, by 1681, in the seventeenth century, 300 years ago.*

- *By 1681,* he had many students.
- He lived *in the seventeenth century*.
- He died more than *300 years ago*.

---

3. REMEMBER: the simple past tense of **regular verbs** is formed by adding *–d* or *–ed*.

▶ **BE CAREFUL!** There are often <u>spelling changes</u> when you add *-d* or *-ed* to the verb.

BASE FORM		SIMPLE PAST
live	→	live**d**
join	→	join**ed**
travel	→	travel**ed**
want	→	want**ed**
study	→	stud**ied**
hop	→	hop**ped**
prefer	→	prefer**red**

REFERENCE NOTE
For **spelling rules** for the simple past tense of regular verbs, see Appendix 17 on page A-7.
For **pronunciation rules** for the simple past tense of regular verbs, see Appendix 23 on page A-10.

---

4. Many common English verbs are **irregular.** Their past tense is not formed by adding *-d* or *-ed*.

(See Appendix 1, page A-1, for a list of irregular verbs.)

BASE FORM		SIMPLE PAST
be	→	**was / were**
build	→	**built**
choose	→	**chose**
have	→	**had**
get	→	**got**
go	→	**went**

FOCUSED PRACTICE

 DISCOVER THE GRAMMAR

Read more about Basho. Underline all the verbs in the past tense.
Then complete the time line on the left.

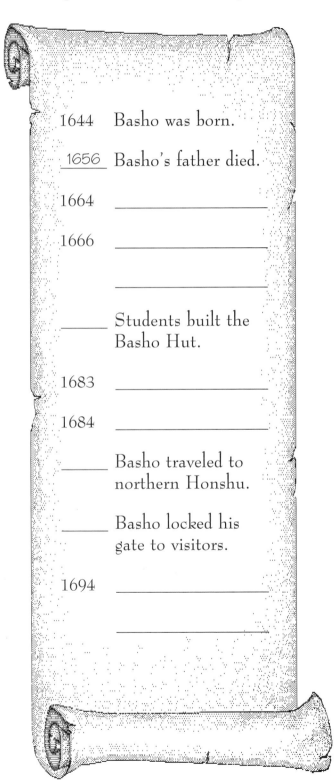

1644 Basho was born.

1656 Basho's father died.

1664 _____

1666 _____

_____ Students built the
         Basho Hut.

1683 _____

1684 _____

_____ Basho traveled to
         northern Honshu.

_____ Basho locked his
         gate to visitors.

1694 _____

       _____

As a son of a samurai, Basho grew up in the household of Todo Yoshitada, a young lord. After his father's death in 1656, Basho stayed on in the Yoshitada household. He and Todo wrote poetry together, and in 1664 they published some poems. Two years later, Todo died suddenly. Basho left the area.

Basho moved around for several years. In the 1670s, he went to Edo and stayed there. He found friendship and success once again. Basho judged poetry contests, published his own poetry, and taught students. His students built him a home outside the city in 1681. They planted a banana tree (a *basho*) in front and called his home Basho Hut. That is how the poet got his nickname: *Basho*.

In spite of this success, Basho became unhappy. He often wrote about loneliness. His mother died in 1683, and he began his travels a year later. His trip to the northern part of Honshu in 1689 was difficult, but his travel diary about this journey, *Narrow Road to the Deep North,* became one of Japan's greatest works of literature.

As a famous poet, Basho had many visitors—too many, in fact. In 1693 he locked his gate for a month, stayed alone, and wrote. The following year he took his final journey, to Osaka. He died there among his friends.

2 ANOTHER POET

Complete this biography of another poet. Use the simple past tense form of the verbs in the boxes.

address appear be become happen lead leave ~~live~~ receive wear write write

Emily Dickinson, one of the most popular American poets,

_____lived_____ from 1830 to 1886. She _____ about
　　　1.　　　　　　　　　　　　　　　　　　　　　2.

love, nature, and time. These _____ her favorite themes.
　　　　　　　　　　　　　　　　3.

Dickinson _____ an unusual life. After just one year
　　　　　　　　4.

of college, she _____ a recluse—she almost never
　　　　　　　　　5.

_____ her house in Amherst, Massachusetts. At home,
　　6.

she _____ visitors, and she only _____ white.
　　7. (negative)　　　　　　　　　　　　　　8.

In addition to her poetry, Dickinson _____ many letters. Other people
　　　　　　　　　　　　　　　　　　　　9.

always _____ the envelopes for her. During her lifetime only seven of
　　　　　10.

her 1,700 poems _____ in print—and this _____ without
　　　　　　　　11.　　　　　　　　　　　　　12.

her knowledge or permission.

Now complete these lines from a poem by Emily Dickinson. Use the simple past tense form of the verbs in the box.

bite ~~come~~ drink eat hop see

A bird _____came_____ down the walk:
　　　　　13.
He did not know I _____;
　　　　　　　　14.
He _____ an angle-worm in halves
　　　15.
And _____ the fellow raw.
　　　16.
And then he _____ a dew
　　　　　　　17.
From a convenient grass,

And then _____ sidewise to the wall
　　　　　　18.
To let a beetle pass.

3 TWO POETS

*Read about Basho. Ask questions about Dickinson. Write **yes / no** questions about the underlined verbs. Write **wh-** questions about other underlined words. Then answer the questions with information from Exercise 2.*

1. Basho <u>was</u> a poet.

   A: Was Dickinson a poet?

   B: Yes, she was.

2. He was born <u>in 1644</u>.

   A: When was Dickinson born?

   B: She was born in 1830.

3. He <u>became</u> famous during his lifetime.

   A: _____

   B: _____

4. Basho <u>received</u> many visitors.

   A: _____

   B: _____

5. He <u>traveled</u> a lot.

   A: _____

   B: _____

6. Basho wrote <u>more than 1,000 poems</u>.

   A: _____

   B: _____

7. He wrote <u>about nature</u>.

   A: _____

   B: _____

8. He died <u>in 1694</u>.

   A: _____

   B: _____

4 ANA CASTILLO

Read the article about a modern writer.

Ana Castillo is a modern poet, novelist, short story writer, and teacher. She was born in Chicago in 1953, and she lived there for thirty-two years. *Otro Canto,* her first book of poetry, appeared in 1977. In her work, she uses humor and a lively mixture of Spanish and English (Spanglish). She got her special writer's "voice" in a neighborhood with many different ethnic groups. She also thanks her father. "He had an outgoing and easy personality, and this . . . sense of humor. I got a lot from him. . . ."

   Castillo attended high school, college, and graduate school in Chicago. In the 1970s, she taught English as a Second Language and Mexican history. She received a Ph.D. in American studies from Bremen University in Germany in 1992.

Read the statements. Write **That's right** *or* **That's wrong**. *Correct the wrong statements.*

1. Ana Castillo was born in Mexico City.

   That's wrong. She wasn't born in Mexico City. She was born in Chicago.

2. She lived in Chicago until 1977.

_____

3. Her father was very shy.

_____

4. She grew up among people of different cultures.

_____

5. Castillo got most of her education in Chicago.

_____

6. She taught Spanish in the 1970s.

_____

7. She went to France for her Ph.D.

_____

COMMUNICATION PRACTICE

5 LISTENING

 *Listen to part of an interview with a poet. Listen again, and write the years on the time line.*

| was born | parents left Turkey | moved to U.S. | began to write poetry | graduated from college | won poetry award | became a teacher |

1970

6 INFORMATION GAP: COMPLETE THE BIOGRAPHY

Work in pairs (A and B). Student B, turn to page 29 and follow the instructions there. Student A, read the short biography below. Ask your partner questions to complete the missing information. Answer your partner's questions.

EXAMPLE:

A: Where was Vladimir born?

B: He was born in Kiev.

When was he born?

A: He was born on May 6, 1975.

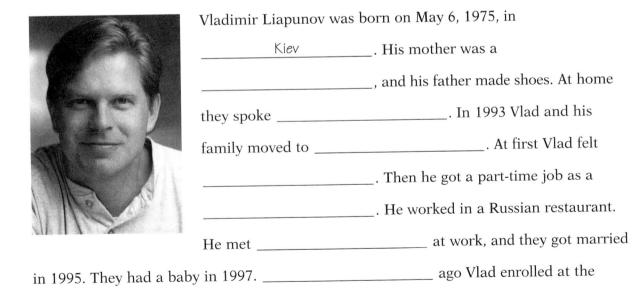

Vladimir Liapunov was born on May 6, 1975, in

_____Kiev_____. His mother was a

_____, and his father made shoes. At home

they spoke _____. In 1993 Vlad and his

family moved to _____. At first Vlad felt

_____. Then he got a part-time job as a

_____. He worked in a Russian restaurant.

He met _____ at work, and they got married

in 1995. They had a baby in 1997. _____ ago Vlad enrolled at the

community college. His goal is to own his own restaurant someday.

When you are finished, compare biographies. Are they the same?

7 DIFFERENT LIVES

Work in pairs. Reread the information about Matsuo Basho (see pages 19 and 23) and Emily Dickinson (see page 24). In what ways were the two poets similar? How were they different? With your partner, write as many ideas as you can. Compare your ideas with your classmates.

EXAMPLES:

A: Both Basho and Dickinson were poets.

B: Basho lived in the seventeenth century. Dickinson lived in the nineteenth century.

8 HAIKU FOR YOU

Work in pairs. Write a three-line haiku poem. Make an observation about nature. Try to use the simple past tense. Share your poem with your classmates.

EXAMPLE:

Early spring petals

Fell on rain-wet ground—

A hint of autumn?

9 RHYMING PAIRS

In poetry the last word of a line sometimes rhymes with the last word of another line. For example, look at these first two lines of a famous poem by Joyce Kilmer. In these lines, **see** *rhymes with* **tree**.

I think that I shall never see

A poem lovely as a tree.

Work with a partner. Write down as many past-tense verbs as you can that rhyme with the verbs in the box.

| sent | bought | drew | kept | spoke |

EXAMPLE:

Sent rhymes with <u>bent</u>, <u>lent</u>, <u>meant</u>, <u>spent</u>, and <u>went</u>.

Compare your lists with those of another pair of students. Who has the most rhyming pairs? Now try to write two lines that rhyme. Use one of the rhyming pairs from the lists you made with your partner. Share your rhymes with your class.

⑩ WRITING

Write a short autobiography. Do not put your name on it. Your teacher will collect all the papers, mix them up, and redistribute them to the class. Read the autobiography your teacher gives you. Then ask your classmates questions to try to find its writer.

EXAMPLES:
Did you come here in 1990?
OR
When did you come here?

INFORMATION GAP FOR STUDENT B

Student B, read the short biography below. Answer your partner's questions. Ask your partner questions to complete the missing information.

EXAMPLE:
A: Where was Vladimir born?
B: He was born in Kiev.
When was he born?
A: He was born on May 6, 1975.

Vladimir Liapunov was born on _____ May 6, 1975 _____,

in Kiev. His mother was a dressmaker, and his father made

_____. At home they spoke Russian.

In _____ Vlad and his family moved to

Boston. At first Vlad felt lonely. Then he got a part-time job as a

cook. He worked in a _____. He met Elena

at work, and they got married in _____.

They had a baby in _____. A month ago Vlad

enrolled at the _____. His goal is to own his own restaurant someday.

When you are finished, compare biographies. Are they the same?

4

USED TO

GRAMMAR **IN CONTEXT**

BEFORE YOU READ Why are jeans so popular throughout the world? What questions can you ask about jeans?

Read this FAQ (Frequently Asked Questions) about blue jeans.

FAQ ABOUT JEANS

◉ *Where are blue jeans from, anyway?*

Gold miners in the California Gold Rush **used to get** a lot of holes in their pants. In the 1850s, Levi Strauss, a recent immigrant from Germany, solved their problem. He used tent material to make extra-strong pants. In this way, the 24-year-old businessman also made his fortune.

◉ *Why do we call them "jeans" and not "strausses"?*

"Jeans" was the name of the strong cotton fabric Strauss used. The material **used to come** mainly from Genoa, Italy. The French called it "gênes" after that city. Today the fabric is called denim, and the pants are called jeans.

◉ *Jeans **didn't use to be** so popular. What happened?*

Jeans **used to be** just work clothes. Then they began to appear on movie stars. James Dean, a 1950s movie actor, **used to wear** jeans. So did Marlon Brando. You know the rest.

◉ ***Did** they **use to come** in so many colors and fabrics?*

No. Blue **used to be** the only color, and denim the only fabric. But not anymore. Today you can buy jeans in many colors and materials. (But they still have to have five pockets or they're not really jeans!)

James Dean

GRAMMAR **PRESENTATION**

USED TO

STATEMENTS

SUBJECT	*USED TO*	BASE FORM OF VERB	
I You He She It We You They	**used to didn't use to**	**be**	popular.

YES / NO QUESTIONS

DID	SUBJECT	*USE TO*	BASE FORM OF VERB	
Did	I you he she it we you they	**use to**	**be**	popular?

SHORT ANSWERS

AFFIRMATIVE		
Yes,	you I he she it you we they	**did**.

SHORT ANSWERS

NEGATIVE		
No,	you I he she it you we they	**didn't**.

WH- QUESTIONS

WH- WORD	*DID*	SUBJECT	*USE TO*	BASE FORM OF VERB
What	**did**	I you he she it we you they	**use to**	**do**?

NOTES

1. Use *used to* + base form of the verb to talk about **past habits** or **past situations** that <u>no longer exist in the present</u>.

Past —X——X——X——X——|———————————— Future
　　　　used to buy　　Now

EXAMPLES

- Lea **used to buy** tight jeans. (*It was her habit to buy tight jeans, but now she doesn't buy tight jeans.*)

(continued on next page)

```
                    Now
Past ─────────────────┼──────────── Future
       └──────────┘   │
        used to hate
```

▶ **BE CAREFUL!** *Used to* always refers to the past. There is <u>no present tense form</u>.

- She **used to hate** loose jeans. *(She hated loose jeans, but now she doesn't hate loose jeans.)*

- In the past, Todd **used to wear** jeans.
  NOT ~~Today Todd uses to wear jeans.~~

---

2. We usually use *used to* in sentences that **contrast the past and the present**. We often emphasize this contrast by using time expressions such as *now, no longer,* and *not anymore* with the present tense.

- Jeans only **used to come** in blue. *Now* you can buy them in any color.
- They **used to live** in Genoa, but they *no longer* live there.
- She **used to wear** a size 6, but she does*n't anymore*.

---

3. BE CAREFUL! Form the **questions** for all persons with ***did + use to***.

Form the **negative** with ***didn't + use to***.

USAGE NOTE: ***Used to*** is more common in affirmative statements than in negative statements or questions.

- **Did** you **use to wear** jeans?
  NOT ~~Did you used to wear jeans?~~
- They **didn't use to come** in different colors.
  NOT ~~They didn't used to come . . .~~

---

4. BE CAREFUL! Do not confuse ***used to*** + base form of the verb with the following expressions:

  –***be used to*** *(be accustomed to)*

  OR

  –***get used to*** *(get accustomed to)*

- I **used to wear** tight jeans.
  (It was my past habit to wear tight jeans.)

- I'm **used to wearing** tight jeans.
  (It is normal for me to wear tight jeans.)

- I can't **get used to wearing** them loose.
  (It still seems strange to me to wear them loose.)

PRONUNCIATION NOTE
Used to and *use to* are pronounced the same: / ˈyustə /

FOCUSED PRACTICE

1 DISCOVER THE GRAMMAR

Read this fashion article. Underline **used to** + *the base form of the verb only when it refers to a habit in the past.*

In many ways, fashion <u>used to be</u> much simpler. Women didn't use to wear pants to the office, and men's clothes never used to come in bright colors. People also used to dress in special ways for different situations. They didn't use blue jeans as business clothes or wear jogging suits when they traveled. Today you can go to the opera and find some women in evening gowns while others are in blue jeans. Even buying jeans used to be easier—they only came in blue denim. I'm still not used to buying green jeans and wearing them to work!

2 TIMES CHANGE

Grammar Note 1

Look at these pictures from an old magazine. Use the verbs in the box with **used to**. *Write one sentence about each picture.*

~~be~~   carry   dance   dress   have   wear

1. Women's skirts _____*used to be*_____ long and formal.

2. All men _____ long hair.

3. Children _____ like adults.

4. Men and women _____ at formal balls.

5. Women _____ many petticoats under their skirts.

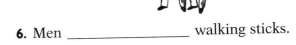

6. Men _____ walking sticks.

3 SNEAKER FAQ

Look at the information about sneakers from 1922. Complete the FAQ. Use the correct form of **used to**.

STYLE	HIGH-TOP	LOW-TOP
MEN'S	98¢	89¢
WOMEN'S	38¢ WHITE	79¢
	95¢ BLACK	
BOYS' AND GIRLS'	85¢ SMALL	73¢ SMALL
	89¢ LARGE	79¢ LARGE
CHILDREN'S	—	65¢

1. Q: _Did sneakers use to come in many colors?_

(sneakers / come in many colors?)

   A: _No. Only in white and black._

2. Q: How many styles did they use to come in?

   A: _____

3. Q: _____

(How much / pair of men's high-tops / cost?)

   A: _____

4. Q: What about women's sneakers? Did they use to cost the same as men's?

   A: _____

5. Q: What kind of sneakers did children use to wear?

   A: _____

6. Q: How many sizes did there use to be for boys and girls?

   A: _____

4 EDITING

Read this student's journal. Find and correct five mistakes in the use of **used to**.
The first mistake is already corrected.

>   use
> When I was younger, clothing didn't ~~used~~ to be a problem. All the girls at my
> school used to wore the same uniform. I used to think that it took away from my
> freedom of choice. Now I can wear what I want, but clothes cost so much! Even blue
> jeans, today's "uniform," used to be cheaper. My mom uses to pay less than $20
> for hers. I guess they didn't used to sell designer jeans back then. You know, I was
> used to be against school uniforms, but now I'm not so sure!

COMMUNICATION PRACTICE

5 LISTENING

Two friends are talking about their teenage years. Listen to their conversation. Listen again. Check the things they used to do in the past and the things they do now.

	Past	Now
1. get up very early without an alarm clock	☑	☐
2. use an alarm clock	☐	☐
3. have a big breakfast	☐	☐
4. have a cup of coffee	☐	☐
5. look at the newspaper	☐	☐
6. have endless energy	☐	☐
7. do aerobics	☐	☐

6 THEN AND NOW

Work with a partner. Look at the photos of pop star Madonna, and read the information about her. Write sentences about Madonna's life in the past, and her life now. Compare your sentences with your classmates' sentences.

Then
- was called Madonna Louise Ciccone
- student, University of Michigan
- sang in bands
- lived in Michigan
- worked in a donut shop

Now
- is called Madonna
- singer, dancer, actress
- sings solo
- owns homes in New York City, Los Angeles, Miami
- has her own music company

EXAMPLE:
She didn't use to wear a lot of makeup.
Now she wears lipstick and eye makeup.

7 THE WAY I USED TO BE

Work in small groups. Bring in a picture of yourself when you were much younger. Talk about the differences in how you used to be and how you are now. What did you use to do? How did you use to dress?

> EXAMPLE:
> I used to wear long skirts. Now I wear short skirts.

8 THIS USED TO BE MY PLAYGROUND

Work with a partner. Read part of the lyrics to a popular song by Madonna. Discuss their meaning.

This used to be my playground
This used to be my childhood dream
This used to be the place I ran to
Whenever I was in need
Of a friend
Why did it have to end?

9 THINGS CHANGE

Work in small groups. Think about how things used to be ten, fifteen, and twenty years ago. Think about the changes in science, business, and your daily life. Share your ideas with each other.

> EXAMPLE:
> A local phone call used to cost ten cents everywhere. Now it costs at least twenty-five cents in most places.

10 WRITING

Write a two-paragraph composition. Contrast your life in the past and your life today. In the first paragraph, describe how your life used to be at some time in the past. In the second paragraph, describe your present life.

> EXAMPLE:
> I used to live in Russia. I attended a university in St. Petersburg. . . .

PAST PROGRESSIVE AND SIMPLE PAST TENSE

GRAMMAR **IN CONTEXT**

BEFORE YOU READ Look at the picture. What do you think happened at "Ligo Diamonds" last Friday night? What was the weather like that night?

Read part of The Alibi, *a radio play.*

[Ding-dong!]

SANDERS: Coming!

OFFICER: Officer Barker. City Police. I'd like to ask you a few questions.

SANDERS: Sure. Sorry I took so long. I **was taking** a shower when the bell **rang**.

OFFICER: Is your wife home?

SANDERS: No, she's at work. Eve's a manager at Ligo Diamonds. She **was** very upset when she **heard** about the burglary.

OFFICER: **Was** your wife **working** that night?

SANDERS: No, she **wasn't**. We **were staying** at Cypress Ski Lodge when it **happened**. Don't tell me we're suspects!

OFFICER: Just for the record, what **were** you and Mrs. Sanders **doing** between 6:00 P.M. and 9:00 P.M. last Friday?

SANDERS: We **were having** dinner in our room.

OFFICER: **Were** you still **eating** at 7:00?

SANDERS: No. My wife **was making** a call from her cell phone.

OFFICER: What **were** you **doing** while your wife **was talking**?

SANDERS: I **was watching** *Wall Street Watch.*

OFFICER: Hmm . . . But the electricity was out because of the blizzard.

GRAMMAR **PRESENTATION**
PAST PROGRESSIVE

STATEMENTS				
SUBJECT	WAS / WERE	(NOT)	BASE FORM OF VERB + -ING	
I	was			
You	were			
He She It	was	(not)	working eating sleeping	yesterday at 7:00 P.M. when Eve **called**. while Sal **was watching** TV.
We You They	were			

YES / NO QUESTIONS			
WAS / WERE	SUBJECT	BASE FORM OF VERB + -ING	
Was	I		
Were	you		
Was	he she it	working eating sleeping	yesterday at 7:00 P.M.? when Eve **called**? while Sal **was watching** TV?
Were	we you they		

SHORT ANSWERS		
AFFIRMATIVE		
	you	**were**.
	I	**was**.
Yes,	he she it	**was**.
	you we they	**were**.

SHORT ANSWERS		
NEGATIVE		
	you	**weren't**.
	I	**wasn't**.
No,	he she it	**wasn't**.
	you we they	**weren't**.

WH- QUESTIONS

WH- WORD	WAS / WERE	SUBJECT	BASE FORM OF VERB + -ING	
Why	**was**	I	**working** **eating** **sleeping**	yesterday at 7:00 P.M.? when Eve **called**? while Sal **was watching** TV?
	were	you		
	was	he she it		
	were	we you they		

NOTES

1. Use the **past progressive** (also called the past continuous) to describe an action that was <u>in progress at a specific time in the past</u>. The action began before the specific time and may or may not continue after the specific time.

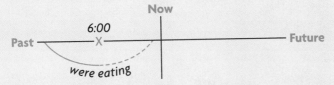

▶ **BE CAREFUL!** Non-action verbs are not usually used in the progressive.
(*See Appendix 2, page A-2, for a list of non-action verbs.*)

2. Use the **past progressive with the simple past tense** to talk about an action that was <u>interrupted by another action</u>. Use the simple past tense for the interrupting action.

Use **when** to introduce the simple-past-tense action OR use **while** to introduce the past-progressive action.

EXAMPLES

- My wife and I **were eating** at 6:00.
- What **were** you **doing** at 7:00?
- They **weren't skiing**.

- I **had** a headache last night. NOT ~~I was having a headache last night.~~

- I **was taking** a shower **when** the phone **rang**.
  (*The phone call came in the middle of what I was doing.*)

- They **were skiing when** the storm **started**. OR
- **While** they **were skiing**, the storm **started**.

(continued on next page)

3. Use the **past progressive with *while*** (or *when*) to talk about <u>two actions in progress at the same time in the past</u>.
Use the past progressive in both clauses.

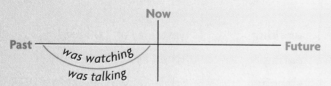

- ***While* I was watching** TV, my wife **was talking** on the phone.

OR

- My wife **was talking** on the phone ***while* I was watching** TV.

4. Notice that the **time clause** (the part of the sentence with *when* or *while*) can come at the <u>beginning or the end</u> of the sentence. The meaning is the same.
Use a comma after the time clause when it comes at the beginning.

- ***When* you called,** I was eating.

OR

- I was eating ***when* you called**.

5. BE CAREFUL! Sentences with both clauses in the simple past tense have a very <u>different meaning</u> from sentences with one clause in the simple past tense and one clause in the past progressive.

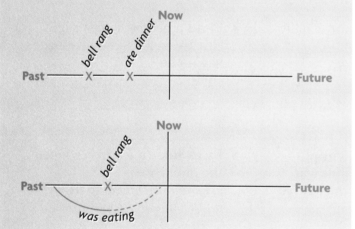

- When the bell **rang, I ate** dinner.
  (First the bell rang; then I ate dinner.)

- When the bell **rang, I was eating** dinner.
  (First I was eating dinner, then the bell rang.)

6. Use the **past progressive** to focus on the <u>duration</u> of an action, not its completion.

- Paul **was reading** a book last night.
  (We don't know if he finished the book.)

Use the **simple past tense** to focus on the <u>completion</u> of an action.

- Paul **read** a book last night.
  (He probably finished it.)

FOCUSED PRACTICE

1 DISCOVER THE GRAMMAR

Circle the letter of the correct answer.

1. In which sentence do we know that the diamond necklace is gone?

   a. He was stealing a diamond necklace.

   (b.) He stole a diamond necklace.

2. Which sentence tells us that the people arrived at the mountains?

   a. They were driving to the mountains.

   b. They drove to the mountains.

3. Which sentence talks about an interruption?

   a. When the phone rang, he answered it.

   b. When the phone rang, he was looking for the safe.

4. Which sentence talks about two actions that were in progress at the same time?

   a. While the officer was questioning Sal, Eve was leaving town.

   b. When the officer questioned Sal, Eve left town.

5. In which sentence did the friends arrive before lunch began?

   a. When our friends arrived, we were eating lunch.

   b. When our friends arrived, we ate lunch.

2 DESCRIBE THE SUSPECTS

Grammar Note 1

Look at the picture of the suspects in last Friday afternoon's burglary. Write about them. Use the past progressive.

1. He ___was wearing a hat.___
            (wear / a hat)

2. She ___wasn't wearing a hat.___
            (wear / a hat)

3. They _____
            (wear / sunglasses)

4. They _____
            (wear / gloves)

5. She _____
            (smile)

6. She _____
            (hold / a cell phone)

7. They _____
            (sit / outside)

8. They _____
            (eat)

3 A TRAFFIC ACCIDENT

Complete the conversation with the simple past tense or the past progressive form of the verbs in parentheses.

REPORTER: What was the cause of the accident, Officer?

OFFICER: Well, it looks like there were many causes. First of all, when the accident

_____occurred_____, the driver _____was driving_____ much too fast. The driver
　　　　1. (occur)　　　　　　　　　　2. (drive)

is a suspect in a burglary, and she _____ town. While she
　　　　　　　　　　　　　　　　　　3. (leave)

_____, she _____ to someone on her car phone.
　　4. (drive)　　　　　　5. (speak)

When she _____ the pedestrian, she immediately _____
　　　　　6. (see)　　　　　　　　　　　　　　　　　　　　7. (step)

on the brakes, but it was too late. The victim wasn't paying attention, either.

First of all, he didn't wait for the traffic light to change. He _____
　　　　　　　　　　　　　　　　　　　　　　　　　　　　8. (cross)

against a red light when the car _____ him. He _____
　　　　　　　　　　　　　　　　9. (hit)　　　　　　　　10. (not see)

the approaching car because he _____ to his friend. The friend
　　　　　　　　　　　　　　　11. (talk)

wasn't paying attention, either. He _____ an ice cream cone while
　　　　　　　　　　　　　　　　　12. (eat)

he _____ the street. When he _____ the car, he
　　13. (cross)　　　　　　　　　　14. (notice)

_____ to push his friend out of the way, but it was too late.
　15. (try)

REPORTER: How is the victim doing?

OFFICER: Well, when the ambulance _____, he _____ from a
　　　　　　　　　　　　　　16. (arrive)　　　　　17. (bleed)

head wound, but the doctors stopped the bleeding and they think he'll be OK.

4 ANSWER CAREFULLY

The police are questioning another suspect in last Friday's burglary. Read this suspect's answers. Use the words in parentheses and the past progressive or simple past tense to write the police officer's questions.

1. **POLICE:** _What were you doing Friday night?_
　　　　　　　　　　(What / do / Friday night?)

   SUSPECT: I was visiting a friend.

2. **POLICE:** _____
　　　　　　　　　(Who / exactly / you visit?)

   SUSPECT: My girlfriend. I got to her house at 5:30 and drove her to work.

3. **POLICE:** _____
　　　　　　　　　(she / work / at 7:00?)

   SUSPECT: Yes, she was working the late shift.

4. POLICE: _____

(anyone else / work / with her?)

SUSPECT: No. She was working alone.

5. POLICE: _____

(What / you / do / while / she / work?)

SUSPECT: I was reading the paper in her office.

6. POLICE: But there was a terrible blizzard Friday night. The lights went out.

_____

(What / do / when / lights go out?)

SUSPECT: I was still reading the paper.

7. POLICE: _____

(What / do / when / lights go out?)

SUSPECT: When the lights went out, we left the building.

8. POLICE: _____

(Why / run / when / the police / see you?)

SUSPECT: We were running because we wanted to get out of the storm.

---

5 **BLIZZARD** Grammar Notes 1–6

Combine these pairs of sentences. Use the simple past tense or the past progressive form of the verb. Remember to use commas when necessary.

1. The blizzard started.   Mr. Ligo attended a party.

When   _the blizzard started, Mr. Ligo was attending a party._

2. It began to snow.   The electricity went out.

When _____

3. He drove home.   He listened to his car radio.

While _____

4. He pulled over to the side of the road.   The visibility got very bad.

_____ when _____

5. He listened to the news.   He heard about the burglary.

While _____

6. The police began the investigation.   It snowed.

_____ while _____

7. It stopped snowing.   Mr. Ligo went to the police station.

When _____

COMMUNICATION PRACTICE

6 LISTENING

The police are trying to draw a detailed picture of an accident. Listen to a witness describe the accident. Then listen again. According to the witness, which set of pictures is the most accurate? Circle the number.

1.

2.

3.

7 ROLE PLAY: THE REAL STORY

Work in groups of four. Follow these steps:

1. Three students are witnesses; the fourth is a police officer. Look at the pictures above.

2. The police officer asks the witnesses questions to describe the accident.

3. Each of the witnesses chooses one set of pictures to describe.

> **EXAMPLE:**
>
> **A:** Can you describe the accident? **A:** Were they paying attention?
>
> **B:** Yes. Two men were crossing the street. **B:** No, they weren't; they were talking.

8 WHAT'S YOUR ALIBI?

Work in small groups. Reread the alibi in the story on page 37. Do you think it is a good alibi? Pretend that you are a suspect in the burglary. What were you doing last Friday night between 6:00 and 9:00 P.M.? Give your alibi to the class. The class will decide which alibis are good and which are bad.

> **EXAMPLE:**
>
> I work from midnight until 7:00 A.M., so between 6:00 and 9:00 P.M. I was sleeping.

9 ARE YOU A GOOD WITNESS?

Look at this picture for ten seconds. Close your book and write down what was happening. See how many details you can remember. What were the people doing? What were they wearing?

EXAMPLE:

A man and woman were standing by the fireplace. The woman was wearing . . .

Compare your list with a classmate's.

10 WRITING

Write a description of an event that you witnessed: an accident, a crime, a reunion, a wedding, or any other event. Use the past progressive and the simple past tense to describe what was happening and what happened during the event.

> **EXAMPLE:**
>
> While I was going to lunch today, I saw a wedding party. People were waiting for the bride and groom outside a temple. They were holding bags of rice. When they saw the couple, they . . .

6 FUTURE

GRAMMAR IN CONTEXT

BEFORE YOU READ Look at the picture. Describe the car. What's new about it? What's the same?

Read an article about future transportation.

Highway to the Future

On the road to exciting new changes in car design

By Harry Vroom
SPECIAL TO THE AUTO GAZETTE

Get ready! We're on the road to exciting new changes in car design. How **will** the vehicle of the future **look**? Well, it **will** probably still **have** four wheels, but it**'s going to come** in many more colors and patterns. You**'ll be able to choose** a green and yellow polka-dotted model or **design** your very own personal look! It**'s going to be** environmentally friendly, too. The material **will be** 100 percent recyclable, and the car **will run** on solar energy.

What about speed? The car of the future **will go** a lot faster than current cars. One day, it **will** even **fly**! But it **will** also **be** safe. An electronic shield around the car **will warn** of danger and automatically **avoid** accidents. And you **won't get** lost anymore! You**'ll** just **say** the destination and the car **will give** you directions.

One manufacturer, Smart Transport, Inc., **is holding** a press conference next week. At the conference you**'ll see** actual models of these fantastic new cars. And before very long, you**'ll be able to zip** around town in the real thing! So, full speed ahead to the future! It**'s going to be** a great trip!

GRAMMAR **PRESENTATION**

BE GOING TO FOR THE FUTURE

STATEMENTS

SUBJECT	BE	(NOT) GOING TO	BASE FORM OF VERB	
I	am*			
You	are			
He She It	is	(not) going to	leave	soon.
We You They	are			

*For contractions of *I am, you are,* etc., see Appendix 20, p. A-8.

YES / NO QUESTIONS

BE	SUBJECT	GOING TO	BASE FORM OF VERB	
Am	I			
Are	you			
Is	he she it	**going to**	**leave**	soon?
Are	we you they			

SHORT ANSWERS

	AFFIRMATIVE	
	you	**are**.
	I	**am**.
Yes,	he she it	**is**.
	you we they	**are**.

SHORT ANSWERS

	NEGATIVE	
	you**'re**	
	I**'m**	
No,	he**'s** she**'s** it**'s**	**not**.
	you**'re** we**'re** they**'re**	

WH- QUESTIONS

WH- WORD	BE	SUBJECT	GOING TO	BASE FORM OF VERB
When Why	**are**	you	**going to**	**leave**?

PRESENT PROGRESSIVE FOR THE FUTURE

STATEMENTS

SUBJECT + BE	(NOT) + BASE FORM OF VERB + -ING	
I**'m**	**(not) leaving**	soon.

See page 3 in Unit 1 for a complete presentation of present progressive forms.

(continued on next page)

WILL FOR THE FUTURE

STATEMENTS			
SUBJECT	WILL (NOT)	BASE FORM OF VERB	
I You He She It We You They	will (not)*	leave	soon.

*For contractions of *I will, you will,* etc., see Appendix 20, page A-8.

YES / NO QUESTIONS			
WILL	SUBJECT	BASE FORM OF VERB	
Will	I you he she it we you they	leave	soon?

SHORT ANSWERS		
AFFIRMATIVE		
Yes,	you I he she it you we they	will.

SHORT ANSWERS		
NEGATIVE		
No,	you I he she it you we they	won't.

WH- QUESTIONS			
WH- WORD	WILL	SUBJECT	BASE FORM OF VERB
When	will	you	leave?

THE SIMPLE PRESENT TENSE FOR THE FUTURE

STATEMENTS		
SUBJECT	VERB	
We	leave	Monday at 6:45 A.M.
It	leaves	

See page 3 in Unit 1 for a complete presentation of simple present tense forms.

NOTES	EXAMPLES

1. There are several ways to talk about actions and states **in the future.** You can use:

–*be going to*

• They**'re going to hold** a press conference.

–**present progressive**

• It**'s taking** place next week.

–*will*

• I think I**'ll go**.

–**simple present tense**

• It **starts** at 9:00 A.M. on Monday.

```
                     Now
                      |
                      |        conference
Past ─────────────────|──────────X─────────── Future
                      |
                      |
```

USAGE NOTE: Sometimes only one form of the future is appropriate, but in many cases more than one form is possible.

2. To make **predictions or guesses** about the future, use:

–*be going to*

OR

–*will*

• People **are going to travel** differently.

OR

• People **will travel** differently.

Use *be going to* instead of *will* when there is something in the present that leads to the prediction.

• Look at those cars! They**'re going to crash**!
NOT ~~They'll crash.~~

(continued on next page)

3. To talk about future **intentions or plans**, use:

–be going to

OR

–will

OR

–present progressive

- He**'s going to hold** a conference next week.

  OR

- He **will hold** a conference next week.

  OR

- He **is holding** a conference next week.

a. We often use *will* when we decide something at the <u>moment of speaking</u>.

A: The car show is opening next week.
B: I love new cars. I think **I'll go**.

Will can also be used for making a request. *(See Unit 13.)*

b. We often use the **present progressive** when we talk about future plans that have already been <u>arranged</u>.

- Jana and I **are buying** a new car next week. We've already chosen the model.

4. Use the **simple present** to talk about <u>scheduled future events</u> (such as timetables, programs, and schedules). Verbs such as *start, leave, end,* and *begin* are often used this way.

- The press conference **begins** at 9:00 A.M.
- It **ends** promptly at 9:45.

PRONUNCIATION NOTE
In informal speech, *going to* is often pronounced *gonna* /gɔnə/.

FOCUSED PRACTICE

1 DISCOVER THE GRAMMAR

Read this transcript and listen to a radio interview with Professor Harry Vroom, a well-known researcher of the Future Watch Institute. There are fifteen verb forms that refer to the future. Find and underline them.

INTERVIEWER: For those of you who are just tuning in, this is "Looking Into the Future." I am Will Bee, and we are talking with Professor Harry Vroom. Good afternoon, Professor. I understand you <u>are going to tell</u> our listeners about the cars of the future.

VROOM: That's right. I believe there will be some surprising changes in the next century. Let me give you some examples. Cars of the future are going to have "brains." They'll start themselves, and they'll adjust the seats, mirrors, and steering wheels automatically. Luxury cars will even ask you where you want to go and will tell you the best route to take.

INTERVIEWER: That certainly is amazing! I'm sure lots of our listeners have questions for you, but, unfortunately, we only have time today for a few call-ins.

VROOM: Well, you know, I am speaking at the annual Car Show next week. The show begins at 10:00 A.M. on August 11. I'm going to talk more about the plans for cars of the future. I'm also going to show some models. I hope many of your listeners will be there.

INTERVIEWER: I'm sure they will. We have to pause for a commercial break. But don't go away, listeners. We'll be right back—and Professor Vroom will be ready to answer some of your questions.

2 IT'S GOING TO HAPPEN

Look at the pictures. They show events from a day in Professor Vroom's life.
Write predictions or guesses. Use the words in the box and a form of **be going to**
or **not be going to**.

answer the phone	drive	get very wet	give a speech
have dinner	rain	~~take a trip~~	watch TV

1. ___He's going to take a trip.___

2. _____

3. _____

4. _____

5. _____

6. _____

7. _____

8. _____

3 PROFESSOR VROOM'S SCHEDULE

Write about Professor Vroom's plans for next week. Use the information from his calendar and the present progressive. Add **the** *and* **a** *when necessary.*

	Monday	Tuesday	Wednesday	Thursday	Friday
A.M.	take train to New Haven	go to Washington (8:00 A.M.)	work in research lab all day	attend annual Car Show	talk on radio show
P.M.	give lecture at Yale				

1. On Monday morning _he's taking the train to New Haven._

2. On Monday evening _____

3. On Tuesday morning _____

4. All day Wednesday _____

5. On Thursday morning _____

6. On Friday morning _____

4 RADIO CALL-IN QUESTIONS

Radio listeners are calling in with questions for Professor Vroom. Complete the questions and answers. Use the words in parentheses and **will** *or* **won't**.

CALLER 1: Hello, Professor Vroom. My question is this: _____Will_____ the car of the

future _____run_____ on gasoline?
1. (run)

VROOM: No, it _____. It _____ probably _____
2.   3. (use)

solar energy. Thanks for calling. Next?

CALLER 2: I had a flat tire yesterday. I was wondering, _____ we still

_____ flat tires on these future cars?
4. (get)

VROOM: No, we _____. In fact, by the year 2010, flat tires
5.

_____ a thing of the past. Tires _____ a special seal
6. (be)   7. (have)

so they _____ themselves automatically.
8. (repair)

CALLER 3: Sounds great. In what other ways _____ the car of the future

_____ different?
9. (be)

(continued on next page)

Vroom: Well, instead of keys, cars _____ smart cards. These
10. (have)

_____ a lot like credit cards. They _____ doors,
11. (look)   12. (open)

and they _____ the seats, mirrors, and steering wheels. They
13. (adjust)

_____ even _____ the inside temperature.
                           14. (control)

Caller 3: _____ they _____ prevent car thefts?
                                         15. (help)

Vroom: Yes, they _____! OK, next caller?
                          16.

Caller 4: Hello. I'm curious. How much _____ these cars

_____?
17. (cost)

Vroom: I don't know exactly, but they certainly _____ cheap.
                                                           18. (not be)

---

5 ALL ABOARD

Grammar Note 4

*Professor Vroom is going to take the train from New York to New Haven on
Monday. He is asking questions at the information booth. Write his questions. Then
look at the train schedule and write the answers. Use the simple present tense.*

NEW YORK TO NEW HAVEN					
MONDAY TO FRIDAY, EXCEPT HOLIDAYS					
Leave	**Arrive**	**Leave**	**Arrive**	**Leave**	**Arrive**
New York	**New Haven**	**New York**	**New Haven**	**New York**	**New Haven**
AM	**AM**	**PM**	**PM**	**PM**	**PM**
12:35	2:23	3:22	4:55	6:04	7:46
1:30	3:37	3:37	5:17	6:30	8:16
6:02	7:48	4:02	5:44	7:06	8:51
7:05	8:55	4:07	5:58	7:37	9:28
8:07	9:57	4:22	6:06	8:07	9:55
9:07	10:53	4:35	6:17	9:07	10:55
10:07	11:53	4:45	6:49	10:07	11:55
11:07	12:53	5:02	6:40	11:20	1:08
12:07	1:53	5:13	7:26	12:35	2:23
1:07	2:54	5:18	7:03	1:30	3:37
2:07	3:55	5:35	7:11	——	——
3:02	4:38	5:39	7:55	——	——
PM	**PM**	**PM**	**PM**	**PM**	**AM**

1. When / the first train to New Haven / leave New York?

Vroom: _When does the first train to New Haven leave New York?_

Information: _It leaves New York at 12:35 A.M._

2. How long / the trip to New Haven / take?

Vroom: _____

Information: _____

3. So, what time / the 9:07 train / arrive in New Haven?

VROOM: _____

INFORMATION: _____

4. About how often / trains / depart for New Haven after that?

VROOM: _____

INFORMATION: _____

5. And what time / the last morning train / leave New York?

VROOM: _____

INFORMATION: _____

6 CHOOSE THE FUTURE Grammar Notes 1–4

Two people are traveling to the Car Show. Read their conversation and circle the most appropriate future forms.

JASON: I just heard the weather report.

ARIEL: Oh? What's the forecast?

JASON: It's raining / (It's going to rain) tomorrow.
1.

ARIEL: Oh, no. I hate driving in the rain. And it's a long drive to the Car Show.

JASON: Wait! I have an idea. We'll take / We're going to take the train instead!
2.

ARIEL: Good idea! Do you have a train schedule?

JASON: Yes. Here's one. There's a train that will leave / leaves at 7:00 A.M.
3.

ARIEL: What about lunch? Oh, I know, I'll make / I'm making some sandwiches for us to
4.
take along. I don't like train food.

JASON: Sounds good. You know, it's a long trip. What are we doing / are we going to do all
5.
those hours?

ARIEL: Don't worry. We'll think / We're thinking of something.
6.

JASON: You know, we have to get up really early.

ARIEL: That's true. I think I'm going / I'll go home now.
7.

JASON: OK. I'm seeing you / I'll see you tomorrow. Good night.
8.

COMMUNICATION PRACTICE

7 LISTENING

Listen to the short conversations. Decide if the people are talking about something happening now or in the future. Listen again and check the correct column.

	Now	Future
1.	☐	☑
2.	☐	☐
3.	☐	☐
4.	☐	☐
5.	☐	☐
6.	☐	☐

8 FORTUNE COOKIES

Most Chinese restaurants in the United States give you fortune cookies at the end of your meal. Inside each cookie is a small piece of paper with a prediction about the future.

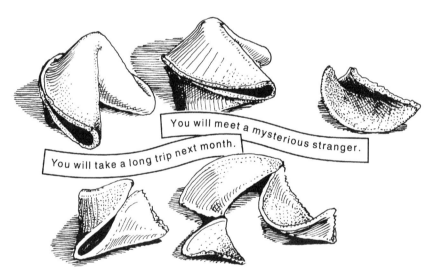

You will meet a mysterious stranger.

You will take a long trip next month.

On a piece of paper, write down a fortune. Now work in small groups. Put all the fortunes in a pile and have each person take one. Discuss your fortunes with the group.

EXAMPLE:

A: "You will take a long trip next month."
That's not possible. I'm starting my new job next week.

B: "You will meet a mysterious stranger."
It's possible. I'm going to a party tomorrow night.

9 WHEN ARE YOU FREE?

Complete your weekend schedule. If you have no plans, write **free**.

	Friday	Saturday	Sunday
12:00 P.M.			
1:00 P.M.			
2:00 P.M.			
3:00 P.M.			
4:00 P.M.			
5:00 P.M.			
6:00 P.M.			
7:00 P.M.			
8:00 P.M.			
9:00 P.M.			

Now work with a partner. Ask questions to decide on a time when you are both free to do something together.

EXAMPLE:

A: What are you doing Friday afternoon? Do you want to go to the movies?

B: I'm studying at the library. How about Friday night? Are you doing anything then?

10 CHOOSE A TIME

Work with the same partner as in Exercise 9. Look at this movie schedule. Then look at your schedules from Exercise 9. Decide which movie to see and when.

Speed *(action)*
  Sun. 12:00, 2:15, 4:30, 6:45, 9:00.
Back to the Future *(science fiction)*
  Fri.–Sun. 2:30, 4:45, 7:00, 8:45.
Strangers on a Train *(mystery)*
  Thurs.–Fri. 5:45, 7:00, 8:15.
Airplane! *(comedy)*
  Fri.–Sat. 4:45, 6:00, 7:15, 9:00.
  Sun. 1:15, 3:00, 4:15, 5:30, 7:15, 9:00.
Taxi Driver *(suspense)*
  Sun. 1:00, 3:00, 5:00.

EXAMPLE:

A: There are three good movies Friday night. *Back to the Future* is playing at 7:00. Is that OK?

B: That's a little early. When does the next show begin?

11 WRITING

Write a paragraph describing the ideal car of the future. Use your imagination. What material will it be made of? What form of energy is it going to use? How fast will it go? What features is it going to have?

7 FUTURE TIME CLAUSES

GRAMMAR **IN CONTEXT**

BEFORE YOU READ Look at the picture. What is the child thinking?

Read this article about setting goals.

GO FOR IT!

What are your dreams for your future?

Are you **going to get** your degree *by the time you're twenty-two*? **Will** you **start** your own business *before you turn forty*? We all have dreams, but they **won't become** reality *until we change them to goals*. Here's how.

■ **PUT YOUR DREAMS ON PAPER.** *When you write a dream down,* it **will start** to become a goal. Your path will be a lot clearer.

■ **NOW LIST BENEFITS.** For example, Latoya Jones **is going to go back** to school *as soon as she saves enough*

money. One benefit: She**'ll get** the job she wants *when she has her degree. When things get tough,* Latoya **will read** her list and **remember** the benefits.

■ **WRITE DOWN SMALLER GOALS.** It's easier to reach a goal when you break it down into steps. *Before Latoya applies,* she's **going to look** at school catalogs. She **won't decide** on a school *until she visits several of them.*

■ **ACT TODAY.** Will you watch TV before dinner tonight or read school catalogs? *After you know your smaller goals,* it **will be** easier to make these small decisions every day.

GRAMMAR **PRESENTATION**
FUTURE TIME CLAUSES

STATEMENTS				
MAIN CLAUSE			**TIME CLAUSE**	
I **will** I **am going to**			I **graduate**	
She **will** She **is going to**	**get** a job	**when**	she **graduates**	next June.
They **will** They **are going to**			they **graduate**	

YES / NO QUESTIONS				
MAIN CLAUSE			**TIME CLAUSE**	
Will I **Am** I **going to**			I **graduate**	
Will she **Is** she **going to**	**get** a job	**when**	she **graduates**	next June?
Will they **Are** they **going to**			they **graduate**	

SHORT ANSWERS		
AFFIRMATIVE		
Yes,	you	**will.** **are.**
	she	**will.** **is.**
	they	**will.** **are.**

SHORT ANSWERS		
NEGATIVE		
No,	you	**won't.** **aren't.**
	she	**won't.** **isn't.**
	they	**won't.** **aren't.**

WH- QUESTIONS					
	MAIN CLAUSE			**TIME CLAUSE**	
Where	**will** I **am** I **going to**			I **graduate**	
	will she **is** she **going to**	**get** a job	**when**	she **graduates**	next June?
	will they **are** they **going to**			they **graduate**	

NOTES

1. When a sentence about future time has two clauses, the verb in the <u>main clause</u> is often in the **future** (*will* or *be going to*). The verb in the <u>time clause</u> is often in the **present tense**.

▶ **BE CAREFUL!** Do not use *will* or *be going to* in a future time clause.

The **time clause** can come at the beginning or the end of the sentence. The meaning is the same. Use a <u>comma</u> after the time clause when it comes at the beginning. Do not use a comma when it comes at the end.

EXAMPLES

main clause   time clause
- He**'ll look** for a job **when he graduates**.

main clause   time clause
- I**'m going to work** *after I graduate*.

NOT ~~when he will graduate.~~
NOT ~~after I will graduate.~~

time clause
- *Before she applies,* she'll visit schools.

OR

time clause
- She'll visit schools *before she applies*.

NOT ~~She'll visit schools, before she applies.~~

2. Here are some **common time expressions** you can use to begin future time clauses.

   a. *When*, *after*, and *as soon as* often introduce <u>the event that happens first</u>.

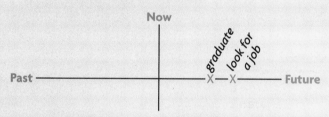

   b. *Before*, *until*, and *by the time* often introduce <u>the event that happens second</u>.

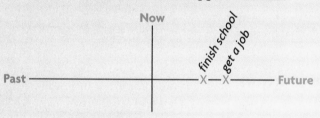

   c. *While* introduces an event that will happen <u>at the same time</u> as another event.

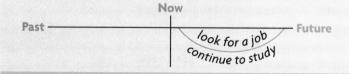

- *When* I graduate, I'll look for a job.
- I'll look for a job *after* I graduate.
- *As soon as* I graduate, I'll look for a job.
  (*First I'm going to graduate. Then I'll look for a job.*)

- *Before* I get a job, I'll finish school.
- I won't get a job *until* I finish school.
- *By the time* I get a job, I'll be out of school.
  (*First I'll finish school. Then I'll get a job.*)

- *While* I look for a job, I'll continue to study.
  (*I will look for a job and study during the same time period.*)

FOCUSED PRACTICE

1 DISCOVER THE GRAMMAR

Read the first sentence in each set. Then circle the letter of the sentences whose meaning is similar.

1. Amber will open her own business when she finishes school.
   a. Amber will open her own business. Then she'll finish school.
   b. Amber will finish school. Then she'll open her own business.

2. Denzell won't quit until he finds another job.
   a. Denzell will find another job. Then he'll quit.
   b. Denzell will quit. Then he'll find another job.

3. Jake will retire as soon as he turns sixty.
   a. Jake will retire. Then he'll turn sixty.
   b. Jake will turn sixty. Then he'll retire.

4. After the Morrisons sell their house, they'll move to Florida.
   a. The Morrisons will sell their house. Then they'll move to Florida.
   b. The Morrisons will move to Florida. Then they'll sell their house.

5. Marisa will call you when she gets home.
   a. Marisa will call you. Then she'll get home.
   b. Marisa will get home. Then she'll call you.

6. Demetri and Iona are going to look for an apartment before they get married.
   a. Demetri and Iona are going to get married. Then they'll look for an apartment.
   b. Demetri and Iona are going to look for an apartment. Then they'll get married.

7. While Li-jing is in school, she'll work part-time.
   a. Li-jing will finish school. Then she'll get a part-time job.
   b. Li-jing will go to school. At the same time she'll have a part-time job.

8. By the time Marta gets her diploma, she'll be twenty-one.
   a. Marta will get her diploma. Then she'll turn twenty-one.
   b. Marta will turn twenty-one. Then she'll get her diploma.

2 WHAT'S NEXT?   Grammar Notes 1–2

Combine these sentences.

1. Sandy and Jeff will get married. Then Sandy will graduate.

   ___Sandy and Jeff will get married___ before ___Sandy graduates.___

2. Jeff is going to get a raise. Then they are going to move to a larger apartment.

   _____ as soon as _____

3. They're going to move to a larger apartment. Then they're going to have a baby.

   After _____

(continued on next page)

4. They'll have their first child. Then Sandy will get a part-time job.

_____ after _____

5. Their child will be two. Then Sandy will go back to work full-time.

By the time _____

6. Sandy will work full-time, and Jeff will go to school.

_____ while _____

7. Jeff will graduate. Then he'll find another job.

_____ when _____

3 **LOOKING AHEAD**

Complete this student's worksheet. Use the correct form of the verbs in parentheses.

GOAL PLANNING WORKSHEET

I. Write your major goal.

I ___'ll get___ a job after I _____.
    (get)   (graduate)

II. List three benefits of achieving your goal.

1. When I _____ a job, I _____ more money.
         (get)   (have)

2. When I _____ enough money, I _____ a used car.
        (save)   (buy)

3. I _____ happier when I _____ employed.
    (feel)   (be)

III. How will you reach your goal? Write down smaller goals.

1. As soon as I _____ in the morning, I _____ the
        (get up)   (buy)
newspaper to look at the employment ads.

2. When I _____ to my friends, I _____ them if they
        (speak)   (ask)
know of any jobs.

3. I _____ at the job notices board when I _____ to the
    (look)   (go)
supermarket.

4. Before I _____ on an interview, I _____ my
        (go)   (improve)
computer skills.

COMMUNICATION PRACTICE

4 LISTENING

A woman is calling Jobs Are Us Employment Agency. Listen. Read the sentences that follow. Then listen again and number the events in order.

_____ **a.** speak to a job counselor   _____ **d.** receive more job training

_____ **b.** have interview at the agency   _____ **e.** go to companies

__1__ **c.** send a resume   _____ **f.** take a word-processing test

5 THE NEXT STEP

Fill out this questionnaire. Check (✓) the appropriate boxes.

When I finish this course, I'm going to . . .

☐ take another English course.   ☐ take some time off.

☐ apply to another school.   ☐ go on vacation.

☐ look for a new job.   ☐ Other: _____

Now work in a small group. Take a survey. What are your classmates going to do when they finish this course? Compare your group's answers with the other groups' answers.

> EXAMPLE:
> **A:** Ten students are going to take another English course when they finish this course.
> **B:** Two students are going to look for a new job.

6 UNTIL THEN

Complete these three sentences. Then compare your answers with your classmates' answers. How many different answers are there? Remember that all sentences refer to future time.

a. I'm going to continue studying English until _____

b. While I'm in this class, _____

c. I'll stay in this country until _____

> EXAMPLE:
> I'm going to continue studying English until I pass the TOEFL® exam.

7 INTERVIEW

Work with a partner. Interview him or her about some future plans. Ask questions such as:

What will you do when . . . ?

Where will you go after . . . ?

Will you . . . while you . . . ?

Take notes and then write a short paragraph about your classmates' plans.

> **EXAMPLE:**
>
> Soo Mi is going to get married next year. Before she gets married, she's going to return home to visit her family. While she's away she'll miss her boyfriend, but she'll write to him every day.

8 WRITING

Complete this worksheet for yourself. Use future time clauses.

GOAL PLANNING WORKSHEET

I. Write your major goal.

I _____

II. List three benefits of achieving your goal.

1. _____

2. _____

3. _____

III. How will you reach your goal? Write down smaller goals.

1. _____

2. _____

3. _____

4. _____

WH- QUESTIONS: SUBJECT AND PREDICATE

GRAMMAR **IN CONTEXT**

BEFORE YOU READ Look at the photograph. Where is the man? What is he doing?

A lawyer is questioning a crime witness. Read part of the court transcript.

STATE OF ILLINOIS V. HAROLD M. ADAMS   March 31, 2000

LAWYER: **What happened on the night of May 12?** Please tell the court.
WITNESS: I went to Al's Grill.
LAWYER: **Who did you see there?**
WITNESS: I saw one of the defendants.
LAWYER: **Which one did you see?**
WITNESS: It was that man.
LAWYER: Let the record show that the
         witness is pointing to the
         defendant, Harry Adams.
         OK, you saw Mr. Adams.
         Did he see you?
WITNESS: No, he didn't see me.
LAWYER: But somebody saw you.
         Who saw you?
WITNESS: A woman. He was talking to
         a woman. She saw me.
LAWYER: OK. **What happened next?**
WITNESS: The woman gave him a package.
LAWYER: A package! **What did it look like?**
WITNESS: It was about this long . . .
LAWYER: So, about a foot and a half. **What did Mr. Adams do then?**
WITNESS: He took the package. He looked frightened.
LAWYER: **Why did he look frightened? What was in the package?**
WITNESS: I don't know. He didn't open it. He just took it and left in a hurry.
LAWYER: **Where did he go?**
WITNESS: Toward the parking lot.
LAWYER: **When did the woman leave?**
WITNESS: She was still there when we heard the explosion in the parking lot.

GRAMMAR **PRESENTATION**
WH- QUESTIONS: SUBJECT AND PREDICATE

QUESTIONS ABOUT THE SUBJECT

WH- WORD SUBJECT	VERB	PREDICATE
Who	**saw**	you?

ANSWERS

SUBJECT	VERB	PREDICATE
He	saw	me.

QUESTIONS ABOUT THE PREDICATE

WH- WORD PREDICATE	AUXILIARY VERB OR *BE*	SUBJECT	VERB
Who(m)	**did**	you	**see?**

ANSWERS

SUBJECT	VERB	PREDICATE
I	saw	**him**.

NOTES

1. Use **wh- questions** (also called information questions) to <u>ask for specific information</u>.

Wh- questions begin with question words such as **who**, **what**, **where**, **when**, **why**, **which**, **whose**, **how**, **how many**, **how much**, and **how long**.

EXAMPLES

- **Who** did you see at Al's Grill?
- **Why** did you go there?
- **How many** people saw you there?
- **How long** did you stay there?

2. When you are **asking about the subject** (usually the first part of the sentence), use a *wh-* question word in place of the subject.

<u>Someone</u> saw you.
- **Who** saw you?

<u>Something</u> happened.
- **What** happened?

---

3. When you are **asking about the predicate** (usually the last part of the sentence), the word order is similar to the word order of a *yes / no* question, but the question begins with a *wh-* word.

You saw <u>someone</u>.
Did you see <u>someone</u>?
- **Who** did you see?

She said <u>something</u>.
Did she say <u>something</u>?
- **What** did she say?

▶ **BE CAREFUL!** When you ask a *wh-* question about something in the predicate, you need either:

a. a form of the verb *be* (*am, is, are, was, were*).

OR

b. an **auxiliary** ("helping") verb such as *do, does, did, have, has, had, can, will*.

- Who **is** Harry Adams?
- Why **was** he at Al's Grill?

- Why **does** she want to testify?
  NOT ~~Why she wants to testify?~~
- When **did** she arrive?
  NOT ~~When she arrived?~~

---

4. USAGE NOTE: In <u>formal</u> English when asking about people in the predicate, **whom** is sometimes used instead of *who*.

FORMAL
- **Whom** did you see?

INFORMAL
- **Who** did you see?

▶ **BE CAREFUL!** If the main verb is a form of *be*, you cannot use *whom*.

- **Who is** the next witness?
  NOT ~~Whom is the next witness?~~

FOCUSED PRACTICE

1 DISCOVER THE GRAMMAR

Match the questions and answers.

___f___ **1.** Who did you see?

_____ **2.** Who saw you?

_____ **3.** What hit her?

_____ **4.** What did she hit?

_____ **5.** Which man did you give the money to?

_____ **6.** Which man gave you the money?

a. His wife saw me.

b. She hit a car.

c. Harry gave me the money.

d. A car hit her.

e. I gave the money to Harry.

f. I saw the defendant.

2 CROSS-EXAMINATION
Grammar Notes 1–4

Complete the cross-examination. Write the lawyer's questions.

1. **LAWYER:** ___What time did you return home?___
   (What time / you / return home?)
   WITNESS: I returned home just before midnight.

2. **LAWYER:** _____
   (How / you / get home?)
   WITNESS: Someone gave me a ride.

3. **LAWYER:** _____
   (Who / give / you / a ride?)
   WITNESS: A friend from work.

4. **LAWYER:** _____
   (What / happen / next?)
   WITNESS: I opened my door and saw someone on my living room floor.

5. **LAWYER:** _____
   (Who / you / see?)
   WITNESS: Deborah Collins.

6. **LAWYER:** _____
   (Who / be / Deborah Collins?)
   WITNESS: She's my wife's boss. I mean, she *was* my wife's boss. She's dead now.

7. **LAWYER:** _____
   (What / you / do?)
   WITNESS: I called the police.

8. **LAWYER:** _____
                                    (When / the police / arrive?)

   WITNESS: In about ten minutes.

9. **LAWYER:** _____
                            (How many police officers / come?)

   WITNESS: I don't remember. Why?

   LAWYER: I'm asking the questions here. Please just answer.

---

❸ Q AND A   Grammar Notes 1–4

Read the answers. Then ask questions about the underlined words.

1. <u>The witness</u> recognized Harry Adams.

   Who recognized Harry Adams?

2. The witness recognized <u>Harry Adams</u>.

   _____

3. Court begins <u>at 9:00 A.M.</u>

   _____

4. <u>Five</u> witnesses testified.

   _____

5. The jury found Adams guilty <u>because he didn't have an alibi</u>.

   _____

6. <u>Something horrible</u> happened.

   _____

7. The trial lasted <u>two weeks</u>.

   _____

8. <u>The judge</u> spoke to the jury.

   _____

9. Adams paid his lawyer <u>$2,000</u>.

   _____

10. The district attorney questioned <u>the restaurant manager</u>.

   _____

COMMUNICATION PRACTICE

4 LISTENING

You are on the phone with a friend. There is a bad connection. Listen to the following sentences. Then listen again. Circle the letter of the question you need to ask in order to get the correct information.

1. a. Who did you see at the restaurant?
b. Who saw you at the restaurant?

2. a. Which car did the truck hit?
b. Which car hit the truck?

3. a. When did it happen?
b. Why did it happen?

4. a. Whose mother did you call?
b. Whose mother called you?

5. a. Who did you report it to?
b. Who reported it?

6. a. How many people heard the shouts?
b. How many shouts did you hear?

7. a. Who saw the man?
b. Who did the man see?

8. a. Why do you have to hang up?
b. When do you have to hang up?

5 WHAT HAPPENED NEXT?

Work with a partner. Look at the court transcript on page 65 again. Read it aloud. Then continue the lawyer's questioning of the witness.

EXAMPLE:

LAWYER: When did the woman leave?

WITNESS: She was still there when we heard the explosion in the parking lot.

LAWYER: What happened next?

6 STAR REPORTERS

Work in small groups. You are going to interview a ten-year-old child genius who is attending law school. You have five minutes to think of as many wh- *questions as you can. One student should write down all the questions.*

EXAMPLES:

When did you decide to become a lawyer?

Who influenced you to become a lawyer?

You will be allowed to ask only six questions. Choose the six best questions. Compare questions with the rest of the class. Now work in pairs. Role-play the interview. Use the six questions your group chose. Then write up the interview for a magazine article.

INFORMATION GAP: POLICE CRIME BOARD

*Two detectives are investigating a case. All the suspects work at the same office.
The detectives interviewed Mary Rogers, the office manager, and wrote her
answers on a board. Work in pairs (A and B). Student B, look at the Information
Gap on p. 72. Student A, look at the chart below. Ask your partner for the
information you need to complete the chart. Answer your partner's questions.*

EXAMPLE:

A: Who did she see at 8:00 P.M.?

B: Rick Simon. Where did she see him?

A: At Al's Grill. Who else saw him?

Suspect	Time	Location	Other Witnesses
Rick Simon	8:00 P.M.	Al's Grill	
Alice May		Fifth Avenue	Bob May
Jake Bordon	6:30 P.M.		the janitor
	7:15 P.M.		some children
John Daniels	7:00 P.M.		

When you are finished, compare your charts. Are they the same?

 WRITING

*Work with a partner. Think of something exciting or interesting that you once
saw. Tell your partner. Then write a list of questions and interview your partner
to get more information. Write up the interview.*

EXAMPLE:

A: What did you see?

B: It was a famous person in a restaurant.

A: Who was it?

B: . . .

Student B, ask your partner for the information you need to complete the chart.
Answer your partner's questions.

EXAMPLE:

A: Who did she see at 8:00 P.M.?

B: Rick Simon. Where did she see him?

A: At Al's Grill. Who else saw him?

Suspect	Time	Location	Other Witnesses
Rick Simon	8:00 P.M.	Al's Grill	the waiter
Alice May	7:30 P.M.		
Jake Bordon	6:30 P.M.	the office	
Lilly Green	7:15 P.M.	in the park	
		Tony's Pizza	two customers

When you are finished, compare your charts. Are they the same?

REVIEW OR SELFTEST

PART

I

I. *Complete each sentence with the simple present tense or present progressive form of the verb in parentheses.*

1. You ___'re breathing___ hard. Sit down and rest for a while.
      (breathe / are breathing)

2. Dolphins and whales are mammals. They have lungs and they

   _____ air.
      (breathe / are breathing)

3. Fred just left. He _____ to his biology class right now.
      (goes / is going)

4. He _____ to biology class twice a week.
      (goes / is going)

5. In our area, it _____ a lot in March.
      (rains / is raining)

6. It _____ right now, and I don't have my umbrella.
      (rains / is raining)

7. We _____. Is the music too loud for you?
      (dance / are dancing)

8. We _____ every day. It's good exercise.
      (dance / are dancing)

II. *Complete the conversations with short answers and the present progressive or simple present tense of the verbs in parentheses.*

1. A: _____Are_____ you ____getting____ ready for school? It's 7:45.
                                    1. (get)

   B: Yes, I _____am_____ . I _____ my teeth right now.
                        2.   3. (brush)

   A: How about Sue? _____ she _____ dressed?
                                                          4. (get)

   B: I _____ so. She _____ for her shoes.
             5. (think)   6. (look)

2. A: Something _____ good. What _____ you
                          7. (smell)

   _____ ?
      8. (cook)

   B: Pancakes. Hey, _____ you _____ your book bag?
                                                      9. (have)

   A: No, I _____ . _____ you _____ where it is?
                    10.   11. (know)

   B: You _____ it in your room these days, right?
               12. (keep)

   A: I _____ in my room right now, but I _____ it.
             13. (stand)   14. (not see)

(continued on next page)

3. A: Yuck. This milk _____ awful. I'm going to have juice instead.
15. (taste)

B: Look, I _____ one sandwich for lunch. _____ that enough?
16. (pack)   17. (be)

A: I _____ any lunch. I _____ hungry today.
18. (not want)   19. (not be)

B: You _____ pale. _____ you _____ OK?
20. (look)   21. (feel)

A: Yes, I _____. I'm just a little nervous about my spelling test.
22.

B: Oh, no! Look at the time. I think I _____ the school bus.
23. (hear)

A: Don't worry. We _____ right now.
24. (leave)

B: Bye. Have a great day!

III. *Complete each sentence with a negative or affirmative imperative. Use the verbs in the box. Use some verbs more than once.*

| forget | enjoy | lock | call | walk | have | put |

1. Please _____walk_____ the dog in the morning and afternoon.

2. But _____ her near the Wongs' house. She chases their cat.

3. Please _____ the back door before you go out. The key is in the door.

4. Also, _____ to turn out the lights. We have high electric bills.

5. _____ newspapers in the garbage. They go in the green bin. We recycle them.

6. _____ the garbage cans on the sidewalk on Tuesday morning.

7. _____ me if you have any problems.

8. But _____ after 11:00. We go to bed early when we're on vacation.

9. _____ fun, and _____ the house.

IV. *Complete the conversation with short answers or the simple past tense form of the verbs in parentheses.*

A: Are you from Baltimore?

B: No, I'm not. I _____was born_____ in China, but I _____ here ten years ago.
1. (be born)   2. (move)

A: Where _____ you _____ in China?
3. (live)

B: In Shanghai.

A: Oh, really? I _____ in Shanghai last year. I _____ English
                     4. (be)   5. (teach)
there for three years.

B: That's interesting. _____ you _____ it?
                                     6. (like)

A: Yes, I _____. Very much.
                7.

B: _____ the United States _____ strange to you after China?
                          8. (appear)

A: Yes, it _____. I _____ comfortable in Baltimore for months.
                9.   10. (not be)
For one thing, my students here_____ very polite.
                       11. (not seem)

B: I think it's called reverse culture shock. I _____ uncomfortable when I
                                12. (be)
_____ back to China a few years ago.
     13. (go)

A: _____ you uncomfortable for a long time?
     14. (be)

B: No, I _____. Things _____ to feel normal again after a
              15.   16. (begin)
few weeks.

A: _____ you _____ to feel culture shock in your own culture?
                       17. (expect)

B: No, I _____! But I'll be prepared the next time I visit!
      18.

V. *Circle the correct verbs to complete the conversation.*

A: When you were young, did you use to ate / (eat) in restaurants a lot?
                                 1.

B: No, not that often. We used to cooking / cook dinner at home.
                          2.

A: How about prices? Were / Did they lower when you were a kid?
                    3.

B: They sure were. Here's an example. A movie got used to / used to cost a dollar.
                                    4.

A: Wow! Did you go / went to the movies a lot?
                5.

B: Yes. We were going / went every Saturday afternoon. Hey, how about eating that
                    6.
hamburger?

A: OK—but one last question. Did / Are you like everything better in those days?
                               7.

B: Nope. In those days, I wasn't having / didn't have you to talk to. I like things much
                      8.
better now.

VI. *Complete the telephone conversation with the simple past tense or past progressive form of the verbs in parentheses.*

A: Hi, I'm glad you're home! No one _____*answered*_____ a few minutes ago.
    1. (answer)

B: I _____ the lawn when the phone _____. What's up?
    2. (mow)   3. (ring)

A: I _____ a little accident with the car. Nothing serious—no injuries.
    4. (have)

B: Oh, that's good. How about the car?

A: It's OK. There _____ much damage. I _____ fast when
        5. (not be)   6. (not drive)

 I _____ the bus.
    7. (hit)

B: The bus! How _____ you _____ that?
                    8. (do)

A: I _____ to find a special radio station, so I _____ attention.
    9. (try)   10. (not pay)

B: _____ you _____ the police?
                    11. (call)

A: No. It _____ right in front of the police station. An officer
        12. (happen)

 _____ before I even _____ out of the car. After they
    13. (appear)   14. (get)

 _____, I _____ the insurance company.
    15. (leave)   16. (call)

B: Well, I'm just glad you're OK.

VII. *Circle the correct verb to complete each conversation.*

1. A: Do you and Nora have plans for the weekend?
   B: Yes, we're going to / 'll go to a concert on Saturday. I just bought the tickets.

2. A: I can't believe I got into medical school.
   B: You are / 'll be a doctor in just a few years!

3. A: Oh, no! I forgot to deposit my paycheck yesterday.
   B: I'll / 'm going to deposit it for you. It's on my way.

4. A: I'm taking the train to Boston tomorrow.
   B: Oh. What time does / did it leave?

5. A: Take your umbrella. It's going to / 'll rain.
   B: Thanks. I didn't listen to the weather report this morning.

6. A: My son is really interested in science fiction.
   B: Maybe he has / 'll have a career in space exploration when he grows up.

7. A: Look at Rachel's face. I think she's going to / 'll cry.
   B: Poor kid. She really wants to come with us today.

8. A: It's almost June. What are we going to / do we do for the summer?
   B: How about summer school?

9. A: <u>Will / Does</u> Mahmoud call back this afternoon?
   B: He promised to call, but he's usually in class all afternoon.

10. A: Should I make a reservation at Dino's for tonight?
   B: It's already arranged. We <u>are / were</u> meeting there at 6:00.

VIII. *Complete the sentences with the correct forms of the verbs in parentheses. Use* will *in one clause of each sentence.*

1. Laila _____will need_____ some new furniture when she _____moves_____.
   a. (need)   b. (move)

2. As soon as you _____ to Oak Street, you _____ the library.
   a. (get)   b. (see)

3. We _____ here tonight until we _____ the report.
   a. (stay)   b. (finish)

4. After Sid _____ next June, he _____ in the city.
   a. (graduate)   b. (live)

5. I _____ the newspaper while I _____ breakfast.
   a. (read)   b. (eat)

6. They _____ a car when they _____ enough money.
   a. (buy)   b. (save)

7. Carmen _____ me before she _____.
   a. (call)   b. (leave)

8. By the time you _____ thirty, there _____ a shuttle
   a. (turn)   b. (be)
   to the moon.

IX. *Complete the conversations with* **Wh-** *questions.*

1. A: _Where did you go_ _____ last night?
      a.

   B: I went to the movies.

   A: Really? _____ with you?
                          b.

   B: Mona did. She goes every weekend.

   A: _____?
                          c.

   B: We saw *Earthquake*.

2. A: You look upset. _____?
                          a.

   B: Nothing happened. I'm just tired.

   A: _____ on the math test?
                          b.

   B: I got an A.

   A: Wow! Big improvement. _____ with?
                          c.

   B: I studied with Ana. It really helped.

X. *Circle the letter of the correct answer to complete each sentence.*

1. What _____? You look fascinated.   Ⓐ B C D
   (A) are you reading   (C) will you read
   (B) do you read   (D) did you read

2. I am reading a history of the Internet. Did you know it _____   A B C D
   in the 1960s?
   (A) begins   (C) began
   (B) 's going to begin   (D) is beginning

3. Jill, please _____ me your e-mail address again. I lost it.   A B C D
   (A) gives   (C) give
   (B) is giving   (D) gave

4. My e-mail address is jillski4@data.com. _____ it again!   A B C D
   (A) Not lose   (C) Aren't losing
   (B) Won't lose   (D) Don't lose

5. How are you, Naruyo? You _____ a little tired these days.   A B C D
   (A) 'll seem   (C) were seeming
   (B) seem   (D) seemed

6. I _____ some evening classes this semester, and I have a lot   A B C D
   of homework.
   (A) 'm taking   (C) 'm going to take
   (B) take   (D) was taking

7. I remember you. You _____ to go to school here.   A B C D
   (A) used   (C) using
   (B) were used   (D) use

8. You have a good memory. I _____ here for only a month.   A B C D
   (A) go   (C) was going to go
   (B) went   (D) 'm going

9. Will you buy an electric car when they _____ available?   A B C D
   (A) will become   (C) became
   (B) are becoming   (D) become

10. I think I _____ until electric cars are really cheap.   A B C D
    (A) waited   (C) wait
    (B) 'll wait   (D) was waiting

11. _____ when it started to rain?   A B C D
    (A) Were you driving   (C) Do you drive
    (B) Are you driving   (D) Will you drive

12. We were having dinner while it _____.   A B C D
    (A) rains   (C) raining
    (B) 's going to rain   (D) was raining

XI. *Each sentence has four underlined words or phases. The four underlined parts of the sentence are marked A, B, C, or D. Circle the letter of the <u>one</u> underlined word or phrase that is NOT CORRECT.*

1. <u>Before</u> I <u>moved</u> to Chicago, I <u>use to</u> <u>live</u> in the country.   A B Ⓒ D
     A   B   C   D

2. We <u>are going to</u> <u>study</u> tonight <u>until</u> we <u>finished</u> the chapter.   A B C D
          A   B   C   D

3. It<u>'s</u> a one-way street, <u>so</u> <u>no</u> <u>turn</u> left here.   A B C D
     A   B   C   D

4. <u>When</u> Sid <u>will graduate</u> next June<u>,</u> he <u>will live</u> in the city.   A B C D
    A   B   C   D

5. <u>Where</u> <u>you went</u> <u>after</u> you <u>left</u> last night?   A B C D
    A   B   C   D

6. Who <u>did</u> <u>saw</u> you <u>while</u> you <u>were leaving</u> the bank?   A B C D
       A   B   C   D

7. <u>Usually,</u> <u>it's raining</u> a lot here every winter, <u>but</u> last year it <u>didn't</u>.   A B C D
    A   B   C   D

8. <u>Were</u> you <u>watching</u> TV <u>when</u> I <u>call</u> you last night?   A B C D
    A   B   C   D

9. You<u>'ll see</u> the bank<u>,</u> <u>when</u> you <u>get</u> to Main Street.   A B C D
      A   B   C   D

10. We <u>didn't hear</u> the doorbell <u>when</u> he <u>arrived</u> because we <u>ate</u>.   A B C D
       A   B   C   D

11. Years <u>ago</u>, I didn't <u>used to</u> like rock music, <u>but</u> now I <u>love</u> it.   A B C D
        A   B   C   D

12. The movie <u>starts</u> <u>at</u> 7:30, so I <u>think</u> I <u>go</u>.   A B C D
          A   B   C   D

13. <u>Are you wanting</u> to <u>go</u> with me, or <u>are you</u> <u>studying</u> tonight?   A B C D
     A   B   C   D

▶ *To check your answers, go to the Answer Key on page 83.*

FROM GRAMMAR TO WRITING
COMBINING SENTENCES with time words

You can often improve your writing by combining two short sentences into one longer sentence that connects the two ideas. The two sentences can be combined by using a time word such as **while, when, as soon as, before, after,** or **until.** The resulting longer sentence is made up of a main clause and a time clause.

EXAMPLE:

I was shopping. I saw the perfect dress for her. ⟶

time clause   main clause

While I was shopping, I saw the perfect dress for her.

The time clause can come first or second. When it comes first, a comma separates the two clauses.

1 *Read this paragraph. Underline all the sentences that are combined with a time word. Circle the time words.*

I always exchange holiday presents with my girlfriend, Shao Fen. Last year, (while) I was shopping for her, I saw an umbrella in her favorite color. As soon as I saw it, I thought of her. I bought the umbrella and a scarf in the same color. When Shao Fen opened the present, she looked really upset. Later she explained that in Chinese the word for "umbrella" sounds like the word for "separation". When she saw the umbrella, she misunderstood. She thought I wanted to end the relationship. Next year, before I buy something, I'm going to check with her sister!

2 *Look at this student's paragraph. Combine the pairs of underlined sentences with time words such as* **when, while, as soon as, before,** *and* **after.** *Use your own paper.*

I usually keep my wallet in my back pocket when I go out. <u>Two weeks ago, I was walking on a crowded street. I felt something.</u> I didn't pay any attention to it at the time. <u>I got home. I noticed that my wallet was missing.</u> I was very upset. It didn't have much money in it, but my credit card and my driver's license were there. <u>I was thinking about the situation. My brother came home.</u> He told me to report it to the police. <u>I called the police. They weren't very encouraging.</u> They said that wallets often get "picked" from back pockets. They didn't think I would get it back. <u>Tomorrow, I'm going to the movies. I'll keep my new wallet in my front pocket.</u>

EXAMPLE:
Two weeks ago, **while** I was walking on a crowded street, I felt something.

3 *Before you write . . .*

- We often say, "Learn from your mistakes." Think about a misunderstanding or a mistake that you experienced or observed. How did your behavior or thinking change because of it?

- Describe the experience to a partner. Listen to your partner's experience.

- Ask and answer questions about your experiences, for example: *When did it happen? Why did you . . . ? Where were you when . . . ? What will you do . . . ?*

4 *Write a draft of your story. Follow the model below. Remember to use some of these time words and include information that your partner asked about.*

when	while	as soon as	before	until

I (OR My friend) always / often / usually / never_____

_____

_____

Last week / Yesterday / In 1998,_____

_____

_____

_____

_____

In the future / Next time, _____

_____

Exchange paragraphs with a different partner. Complete the chart.

a. The writer used time words to connect ideas.   Yes ____   No ____

b. What I liked in the story:

_____

_____

_____

c. Questions I'd like the writer to answer about the story:
(Note: Write only the questions you want to ask.)

Who _____?

What _____?

When _____?

Where _____?

How _____?

(*Other*) _____?

Discuss the chart with your partner. Revise your paragraph according to the chart.

REVIEW OR SELFTEST
ANSWER KEY

I. (Unit 1)
2. breathe
3. 's going*
4. goes
5. rains
6. 's raining
7. 're dancing
8. dance

II. (Unit 1)
3. 'm brushing
4. Is . . . getting
5. think
6. 's looking
7. smells
8. are . . . cooking
9. do . . . have
10. don't
11. Do . . . know
12. 're keeping
   or keep
13. 'm standing
14. don't see
15. tastes
16. 'm packing
17. Is
18. don't want
19. 'm not
20. look
21. Do . . . feel *or*
   Are . . . feeling
22. do *or* am
23. hear
24. 're leaving

III. (Unit 2)
2. don't walk
3. lock
4. don't forget
5. Don't put
6. Put
7. Call
8. don't call
9. Have . . . enjoy

IV. (Unit 3)
2. moved
3. did . . . live
4. was
5. taught
6. Did . . . like
7. did
8. Did . . . appear
9. did
10. wasn't
11. didn't seem
12. was
13. went
14. Were
15. wasn't
16. began
17. Did . . . expect
18. didn't

V. (Units 3 and 4)
2. cook
3. Were
4. used to
5. go
6. went
7. Did
8. didn't have

VI. (Unit 5)
2. was mowing
3. rang
4. had
5. wasn't
6. wasn't driving
7. hit
8. did . . . do
9. was trying
10. wasn't paying
11. Did . . . call
12. happened
13. appeared
14. got
15. left
16. called

VII. (Unit 6)
2. 'll be
3. 'll
4. does
5. 's going to
6. 'll have
7. 's going to
8. are we going to
9. Will
10. are

VIII. (Unit 7)
2. a. get
   b. 'll see
3. a. 'll stay
   b. finish
4. a. graduates
   b. 'll live
5. a. 'll read
   b. eat
6. a. 'll buy
   b. save
7. a. will call
   b. leaves
8. a. turn
   b. 'll be

IX. (Unit 8)
1. b. Who went
   c. What did you see?
2. a. What happened?
   b. What did you get
   c. Who(m) did you study

X. (Units 1–8)
2. C
3. C
4. D
5. B
6. A
7. A
8. B
9. D
10. B
11. A
12. D

XI. (Units 1–8)
2. D
3. C
4. B
5. B
6. A
7. B
8. D
9. B
10. D
11. B
12. D
13. A

*Where a contracted form is given, the long
form is also correct.

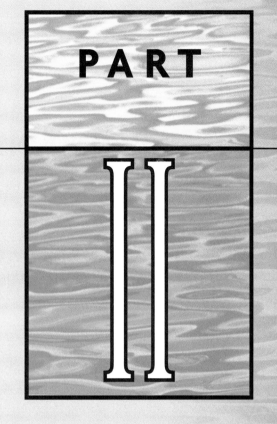

PART

II

PRONOUNS AND PHRASAL VERBS

9

REFLEXIVE AND RECIPROCAL PRONOUNS

GRAMMAR **IN CONTEXT**

BEFORE YOU READ What do you think *self-talk* is? Look at the examples of self-talk in the cartoons. Which are positive? Which are negative?

Read this excerpt from a psychology magazine.

SELF-TALK

IT WAS ALL MY FAULT.

I'LL NEVER FIND ANOTHER JOB.

I'M THE BEST WORKER THEY HAD.

I'LL FIND A BETTER JOB SOON.

Self-talk is the way we explain a problem to **ourselves**. It can affect how we feel and how we act. Take the case of Tom and Sara. They both got laid off from their jobs, but their reactions were very different. Sara frequently called her friends, continued her free-time activities, and kept **herself** fit. Tom, on the other hand, spent all his time **by himself**, didn't allow **himself** to have a good time, and gained ten pounds.

Why were their reactions so different from **one another**? They both lost their jobs, so the situation **itself** can't explain Tom's problems. The main difference was the way Tom and Sara explained the problem to **themselves**. Sara told **herself** that the problem was temporary and that she **herself** could change it. Tom saw **himself** as helpless and likely to be unemployed forever.

Tom and Sara both got their jobs back. Their reactions when they talked to **each other** were, again, very different. For his part, Tom grumbled, "Oh, I guess they were really desperate." Sara, on the other hand, smiled and said, "Well! They finally realized that they need me!"

GRAMMAR **PRESENTATION**

REFLEXIVE AND RECIPROCAL PRONOUNS

REFLEXIVE PRONOUNS			
SUBJECT PRONOUN		**REFLEXIVE PRONOUN**	
I		**myself**	
You		**yourself**	
He		**himself**	
She	looked at	**herself**	in the mirror.
It		**itself**	
We		**ourselves**	
You		**yourselves**	
They		**themselves**	

RECIPROCAL PRONOUNS		
SUBJECT PRONOUN		**RECIPROCAL PRONOUN**
We You They	looked at	**each other**. **one another**.

NOTES

EXAMPLES

1. Use a **reflexive pronoun** when the <u>subject and object</u> of a sentence refer to the <u>same people or things</u>.

(See Appendix 3, page A-2, for a list of verbs and expressions that often take reflexive pronouns.)

- subject = object
  Sara looked at *herself* in the mirror. *(Sara looked at her own face.)*

- subject = object
  They felt proud of *themselves*. *(They were proud of their own actions.)*

2. In **imperative sentences** with reflexive pronouns, use:

–yourself when <u>the subject is singular</u>.

–yourselves when <u>the subject is plural</u>.

REMEMBER: In imperative sentences, the <u>subject is *you*</u>, and *you* can be either singular or plural.

- "Don't push *yourself* so hard, **Tom**," Sara said.

- "Don't push *yourselves* so hard, **guys**," Sara said.

(continued on next page)

3. Use a **reflexive pronoun** to emphasize a noun. In this case, the reflexive pronoun usually follows the noun directly.

- Tom was upset when he lost his job. The **job** *itself* wasn't important to him, but he needed the money.
  (Tom didn't care about the job; he just needed the money.)

---

4. *By* + **a reflexive pronoun** means *alone* or *without any help*.

- Sara lives **by** *herself*.
  (Sara lives alone.)
- We painted the house **by** *ourselves*.
  (No one helped us.)

Be + **a reflexive pronoun** means *act in the usual way*.

- Just **be** *yourself* at your interview.
- He **wasn't** *himself* after he lost his job.

---

5. Use a **reciprocal pronoun** when the subject and object of a sentence refer to the <u>same people</u>, and these people have a <u>two-way relationship</u>.

subject = object
- **Tom and Sara** met *each other* at work.
  (Tom met Sara, and Sara met Tom.)

subject = object
- **We all** told *one another* about our jobs.
  (Each person exchanged news with every other person.)

USAGE NOTE: The traditional grammar rule says to use *each other* when the subject refers to two people, and *one another* when the subject refers to more than two people. Most people, however, use *each other* and *one another* <u>in the same way</u>.

- **Sara and Tom** talked to *each other*.
- **Sara and Tom** talked to *one another*.
- **Sara, Tom, Fred, and Jane** talked to *one another*.
- **Sara, Tom, Fred, and Jane** talked to *each other*.

▶ **BE CAREFUL!** Reciprocal pronouns and plural reflexive pronouns have <u>different meanings</u>.

- Fred and Jane blamed *each other*.
  (Fred blamed Jane, and Jane blamed Fred.)
- Fred and Jane blamed *themselves*.
  (Fred blamed himself, and Jane blamed herself.)

---

6. Reciprocal pronouns have <u>possessive forms</u>: *each other's, one another's*.

- Tom and Sara took *each other's* telephone number.
  (Tom took Sara's phone number, and Sara took Tom's.)

FOCUSED PRACTICE

1 DISCOVER THE GRAMMAR

Read the rest of the article about self-talk. Underline the reflexive pronouns once and the reciprocal pronouns twice. Draw an arrow to the words that these pronouns refer to.

SELF-TALK
continued

Positive self-talk can make the difference between winning and losing. Many athletes use self-talk to help themselves succeed. For example, golf pro Jack Nicklaus used to imagine himself making a winning shot just before he played. Olympic swimmer Summer Sanders prepares herself for a race by smiling.

One sports psychologist believes that Olympic athletes are not very different from one another— they are all the best in their sports. When two top athletes compete against each other, the winner is the one with the most powerful positive "mental movies."

Psychologists say that ordinary people themselves can use these techniques as well. We can create "mental movies" to help ourselves succeed in difficult situations.

2 THE OFFICE PARTY
Grammar Notes 1–2, 4–5

Tom and Sara's company had an office party. Choose the correct reflexive or reciprocal pronouns to complete the conversations.

1. A: Listen guys! The food and drinks are over here. Please come and help

   _____yourselves_____.
   (yourselves / themselves)

   B: Thanks. We will.

2. A: Isn't that the new head of the accounting department over there?

   B: I think so. Let's go over and introduce _____.
   (himself / ourselves)

3. A: I'm really nervous about my date with Nicole after the party. I cut

   _____ twice while shaving, and then I lost my car keys.
   (herself / myself)

   B: Come on. This is a party. Just relax and be _____. You'll do fine.
   (yourself / yourselves)

4. A: What are you giving your boss for the holidays this year?

   B: We always give _____ the same holiday gifts. Every year I give him
   (ourselves / each other)

   a book and he gives me a scarf.

(continued on next page)

5. A: What do you think of the new computer program?

    B: I'm not sure. In our department, we're still teaching _____ how
                                           (ourselves / themselves)
       to use it.

6. A: Jessica looks upset. Didn't she get a promotion?

    B: No, and she keeps blaming _____. I'll lend her that article
                                     (herself / himself)
       about self-talk.

7. A: The Aguayos are going to Japan on vacation this year.

    B: Are they going by _____ or with a tour group?
                          (each other / themselves)

8. A: This was a great party.

    B: Yeah. We really enjoyed _____.
                        (ourselves / myself)

3 WE LEARN FROM ONE ANOTHER   Grammar Notes 1–6

*Read this interview with George Prudeau, a high-school French teacher. Complete
the interview with the correct reflexive or reciprocal pronouns.*

INTERVIEWER: What do you like best about your profession?

GEORGE: One of the great things about teaching is the freedom I have. I run the class

by _____myself_____—just the way I want to. I also like the way my
          1.

students and I learn from _____. My students teach me a lot.
                         2.

INTERVIEWER: What about discipline? Is that a problem?

GEORGE: We have just a few rules. I tell my students, "Keep _____ busy.
                                                 3.

Discuss the lessons, but don't interfere with _____'s work."
                                        4.

INTERVIEWER: What do you like to teach best?

GEORGE: I love French, but the subject _____ really isn't that important.
                                     5.

A good teacher helps students learn by _____ and encourages
                                   6.

them not to give up when they have problems. For instance, John, one of

my students, just taught _____ how to bake French bread. The
                                7.

first few loaves were failures. I encouraged him to use positive self-talk, and

in the end he succeeded.

INTERVIEWER: What teaching materials do you use?

GEORGE: Very simple ones. I pride _____ on the fact that I can teach
8.

anywhere, even on a street corner.

INTERVIEWER: What do you like least about your job?

GEORGE: The salary. I teach French culture, but I can't afford to travel to France.

I have to satisfy _____ with trips to French restaurants!
9.

---

4 **EDITING**

Read this woman's diary. Find and correct six mistakes in the use of reflexive and reciprocal pronouns. The first mistake is already corrected.

Thursday

Jan's birthday was Wednesday, and I forgot to call him.

         myself

I reminded me all day, and then I forgot anyway! I felt

terrible. My sister Anna said, "Don't be so hard on

yourselves," but I didn't believe her. She prides herself

on remembering everything. Then I remembered the

article on self-talk. It said that people can change the

way they explain problems to theirselves. Well, I listened

to the way I talked to me, and it sounded really

insulting—like the way our high school math teacher

used to talk to us. I thought, Jan and I are good friends,

and we treat each other well. In fact, he forgave

myself for my mistake right away. And I forgave him for

forgetting our dinner date two weeks ago. Friends can

forgive themselves, so I guess I can forgive myself.

COMMUNICATION PRACTICE

5 LISTENING

Listen to the conversations at an office party. Then listen again and circle the pronouns that you hear.

1. **A:** Mark's department did a great job this year.

   B: I know. They're really proud of <u>themselves</u> / <u>(each other)</u>.

2. **A:** What's wrong? You look upset.

   B: I just heard Ed and Jeff talking. You know Ed blames <u>him</u> / <u>himself</u> for everything.

3. **A:** I hear you're going to Japan on vacation this year. Are you going by <u>yourself</u> / <u>yourselves</u> or with a tour?

   B: Oh, with a tour.

4. **A:** Hillary looks happy tonight. Did Meredith give her the promotion?

   B: No, not yet. Meredith keeps asking <u>herself</u> / <u>her</u> if she can do the job.

5. **A:** How do you like the new computer system?

   B: I'm not sure. In our department, we're still teaching <u>each other</u> / <u>ourselves</u> how to use it.

6. **A:** So long, now. Thanks for coming. It was good to see you.

   B: Oh, it was a great party.

   A: I'm glad you enjoyed <u>yourself</u> / <u>yourselves</u>.

6 CHEER YOURSELF UP!

What do you tell yourself in a difficult situation? Work with a partner and discuss each other's self-talk in the situations below. Then report to the class.

- you're going to take a big test
- you're stuck in traffic
- you have a roommate you don't like
- you're going to compete in a sport or other event
- you're having an argument with a friend or relative
- you forgot something important

> **EXAMPLE:**
> **A:** What do you tell yourself when you're going to take a big test?
> **B:** I tell myself that I prepared myself well and that I'll do fine.

⑦ THE OPTIMIST TEST

Test yourself by completing the questionnaire.

Are you an optimist or a pessimist?

What do you tell yourself when things go wrong? Check your most likely self-talk for each situation below. Then find out if you're an optimist or pessimist.

1. Your boss doesn't say good morning to you.
   - [ ] **a.** She isn't herself today.
   - [ ] **b.** She doesn't like me.

2. Your family forgets your birthday.
   - [ ] **a.** Next year we should keep in touch with one another more.
   - [ ] **b.** They only think about themselves.

3. You gain ten pounds.
   - [ ] **a.** I promise myself to eat properly from now on.
   - [ ] **b.** Diets never work for me.

4. Your romantic partner decides to go out with other people.
   - [ ] **a.** We didn't spend enough time with each other.
   - [ ] **b.** We're wrong for each other.

5. You're feeling tired lately.
   - [ ] **a.** I pushed myself too hard this week.
   - [ ] **b.** I never take care of myself.

6. Your friend forgets an appointment with you.
   - [ ] **a.** He sometimes forgets to read his appointment book.
   - [ ] **b.** He never reminds himself about important things.

Score you questionnaire . . .
Optimists see bad situations as temporary or limited. Pessimists see them as permanent. All the **a** answers are optimistic, and all the **b** answers are pessimistic. Give yourself 0 for every **a** answer and 1 for every **b** answer.

If You Scored	You Are
0–2	very optimistic
3–4	somewhat optimistic
5–6	pessimistic

Now interview five classmates and find out how they answered the questions. Report the results to another group. Use reflexive and reciprocal pronouns in your descriptions.

EXAMPLE:
For Question 5, three people said they pushed themselves too hard.
Two people said they never take care of themselves . . .

8 THE MEMORY GAME

Work with a partner. First look at the picture carefully for thirty seconds. Then shut your books. Tell each other as many things as you can remember about what people in the picture are doing. Use reciprocal and reflexive pronouns in your description. Take notes. When you are finished, open your books and check your answers. Who remembered the most?

> **EXAMPLE:**
>
> **A:** Two men are waving at each other.
>
> **B:** No, I think the people waving at each other are women.

9 WRITING

Imagine you receive a letter from a friend who attends school in another city. Your friend is not doing well at school and is having problems with a boyfriend or girlfriend. Write your friend a letter. Explain the kind of self-talk you use when things are not going well.

> **EXAMPLE:**
>
> Dear Annette,
>
>   I'm sorry you are having problems in school. Here's what I tell myself when I have problems . . .

PHRASAL VERBS

GRAMMAR **IN CONTEXT**

BEFORE YOU READ Look at the photograph. What kind of work do you think the man does?

 Read this article about Dr. Eloy Rodriguez.

PLANTING IDEAS ∿

*A*s a child, Eloy Rodriguez picked cotton to help support his family. He also **picked up** an interest in plants. Now a famous scientist, Dr. Rodriguez is still interested in plants. Every summer he **takes off** his lab coat, **puts on** his mosquito repellent, and travels to the Amazon region of Venezuela with his students. There, they search for medicinal plants.

Rodriguez **grew up** in Texas. The adults in his large family (sixty-seven cousins lived nearby) **brought** their children **up** to be honest, fair, and *vivo,* or quick-thinking. These values **helped** him **out** in high school. His counselor tried to **talk** him **into** a career in auto mechanics. Rodriguez, however, loved chemistry and went to college instead. He took a job there **cleaning up** a laboratory. He became a science major and then **went on** to graduate school. Soon he was managing the lab.

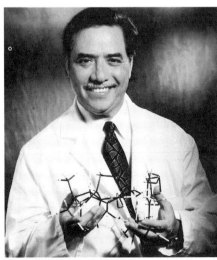

Eloy Rodriguez and anthropologist Richard Wrangham once noticed that sick animals often **pick out** plants to use as medicine. They **turned** their observations **into** a new area of science —zoopharmacognosy. Today Rodriguez is one of the most brilliant scientists in the United States. Rodriguez thanks his family. He **points out** that sixty-four of his cousins graduated from college, eleven with advanced degrees. "Although poverty was there, family was what helped us **get by** in life."

GRAMMAR **PRESENTATION**

PHRASAL VERBS

SEPARABLE TRANSITIVE PHRASAL VERBS

SUBJECT	VERB	PARTICLE	DIRECT OBJECT (NOUN)
He	**put**	**on**	his lab coat.
	helped	**out**	his students.

SUBJECT	VERB	DIRECT OBJECT (NOUN / PRONOUN)	PARTICLE
He	**put**	his lab coat it	**on**.
	helped	his students them	**out**.

INTRANSITIVE PHRASAL VERBS

SUBJECT	VERB	PARTICLE	
She	**started**	**over**.	
He	**grew**	**up**	in Texas.
They	**got**	**back**	early.

NOTES

1. Phrasal verbs (also called two-part or two-word verbs) consist of a verb and a particle. *On, off, up,* and *down* are common particles.

Verb + Particle = Phrasal Verb

Particles and prepositions look the same. However, particles are part of the verb phrase, and they often change the meaning of the verb.

EXAMPLES

verb + particle
• He **put on** his lab coat.

verb + particle
• She **looked up** the word "zoopharmacognosy."

verb + preposition
• She's **looking up** at the sky.
(She's looking in the direction of the sky.)

verb + particle
• She's **looking up** the word.
(She's searching for the word in the dictionary.)

2. USAGE NOTE: Many **phrasal verbs** and one-word verbs have similar meanings. The phrasal verbs are <u>more informal</u> and much <u>more common</u> in everyday speech.

PHRASAL VERB (informal)	ONE-WORD VERB (more formal)
bring up	raise
figure out	solve
go on	continue
pick out	select
take off	remove
wake up	awaken

3. Phrasal verbs can be transitive or intransitive. **Transitive phrasal verbs** <u>have direct objects</u> (d.o).

Most transitive phrasal verbs are **separable**. This means that when the <u>direct object is a noun</u>, it can come:

   –<u>after</u> the verb + particle

       OR

   –<u>between</u> the verb and its particle.

▶ **BE CAREFUL!** When the <u>direct object is a pronoun</u>, it must come <u>between</u> the verb and the particle.

(See Appendix 4, page A-3, for a list of transitive phrasal verbs and their meanings.)

          phrasal verb   d.o.
- He **set up** <u>an experiment</u>.

         phrasal verb   d.o.
- They **figured out** <u>the problems</u>.

      verb + particle   d.o.
- We **dropped off** <u>Mary</u> at the lab.

          OR

      verb   d.o. particle
- We **dropped** <u>Mary</u> **off** at the lab.

          d.o.
- We **dropped** her **off**.
  NOT ~~We dropped off her.~~

          d.o.
- He **cleaned** them **up**.
  NOT ~~He cleaned up them.~~

REFERENCE NOTE
Some transitive phrasal verbs are inseparable. See *Focus on Grammar: High-Intermediate Student Book,* Unit 12.

---

4. Some phrasal verbs are intransitive. **Intransitive phrasal verbs** <u>do not take objects</u>.

(See Appendix 5, page A-3, for a list of intransitive phrasal verbs and their meanings.)

- Dr. Rodriguez **grew up** in Texas.
- He **stood up** to receive the award.

FOCUSED PRACTICE

1 DISCOVER THE GRAMMAR

Read the article. Underline the phrasal verbs. Circle the direct objects of the transitive phrasal verbs.

In Eloy Rodriguez's elementary school in Edinburg, Texas, teachers passed Chicano* students over for special honors classes and punished them for speaking Spanish. When Rodriguez became the first U.S.-born Chicano biology instructor at his university, he worked eighteen hours a day and slept in his lab. "I was very aware that I was the first this, and the first that, and I knew that some people were waiting for me to slip up." Rodriguez didn't slip up. However, he knows that poor treatment turns students off education. Many of them just give up.

Today, Dr. Rodriguez is passing his own success on. When he became a professor at Cornell University, he set out to find Latino** graduate students. He takes these students with him on many of his trips and works hard to turn them into top scientists. In 1990 he set up KIDS (Kids Investigating and Discovering Science)—a science program for minority elementary school children. They put on white lab coats and investigate science with university teachers who treat them like research scientists. They observe nature and figure out problems. In interviews, Rodriguez always brings up role models. "I saw my first snowflake before I saw my first Chicano scientist," he says. Because of Rodriguez's efforts, many students will not face the same problem.

* Chicano—Mexican-American
** Latino—from a Spanish-speaking country in Central or South America

Read these sentences and decide if they are **True (T)** *or* **False (F)**.

__F__ **1.** In Rodriguez's elementary school, teachers chose many Chicano students for honors classes.

_____ **2.** When Rodriguez became a biology instructor, some people expected him to fail.

_____ **3.** Poor treatment makes minority students less interested in education.

_____ **4.** Today, Rodriguez wants to forget his own success.

_____ **5.** He searches for Latino graduate students for his program at Cornell.

_____ **6.** In 1990, Rodriguez visited a program called KIDS.

_____ **7.** Children in KIDS wear the same lab clothes as the scientists.

_____ **8.** Rodriguez rarely mentions role models.

2 COME ALONG!

Complete the flyer. Choose the phrasal verb from the box that is closest in meaning to the verb in parentheses. Use the correct form of the phrasal verb. Use Appendices 4 and 5 on page A-3 for help.

fill out	find out	get up	hand in	pass up
pick up	set up	~~sign up~~	talk over	work out

Two Weeks in the Amazon! <u>Sign up</u> Now!
1. (register)

The Biology Department is now _____ its summer field trip
2. (preparing)

to the Amazonian rain forest in Venezuela. _____ your
3. (get)

application from the Department Office (Room 215), and _____

it _____ right away. _____ it _____
4. (complete)   **5. (submit)**

by May 1.

Last summer we collected plants and identified them. This summer we

plan to talk to local people and _____ how they use plants in
6. (discover)

traditional medicine. This trip is very challenging. We travel to our camp by

canoe. When there are problems, we _____ them

_____ by ourselves. We _____ very early and we
7. (solve)   **8. (arise)**

work hard. There is also some danger, so _____ the trip

_____ with
9. (discuss)

your families before you

decide. We hope you won't

_____ this
10. (reject)

chance to do important

"hands-on science."

③ FOOD FOR THOUGHT

Circle the correct particle to complete each phrasal verb.

Eat some leaves and call me in the morning

In 1972, Richard Wrangham of Harvard University set (out) / up to study some strange behavior of chimpanzees in Tanzania. According to Wrangham, the chimps get by / up at dawn and look for *Aspilia,* plants with furry leaves. They pick them and swallow them whole. Wrangham's observations brought back / up a question. Chimps clearly hated the taste of *Aspilia.* Why do they pick out / over this plant but pass out / up delicious fruit nearby? Wrangham thought this question over / up for several years. He then asked Eloy Rodriguez to help him in / out with the analysis. Together, they worked on / out the puzzle: *Aspilia* contains an antibiotic. Zoopharmacognosy—the study of how animals "doctor" themselves with plants—was born.

④ IN THE FIELD

Complete these conversations. Use phrasal verbs and pronouns.

1. A: Don't forget to put on your mosquito repellent!

   B: Don't worry! I _____put it on_____ as soon as we got here.

2. A: Can we take off our hats? It's really hot.

   B: Don't _____. They protect you from the sun.

3. A: How do you turn on the generator?

   B: It's easy. You _____ with this switch.

4. A: Did you cover up the leftover food? We don't want the ants to get at it.

   B: Don't worry. We'll _____.

5. A: Is Dr. Rodriguez going to call off the field trip tomorrow?

   B: He'll only _____ if someone gets sick.

6. A: Good night. Oh, can someone wake Mike up tomorrow morning?

   B: No problem. I'll _____.

5 IN THE LAB

Unscramble the words to make sentences. In some cases, more than one answer is possible.

1. on / Put / your lab coats — Put your lab coats on. OR Put on your lab coats.

2. the experiment / Set / up _____

3. out / it / Carry _____

4. down / Sit / when you're done _____

5. to page 26 / on / Go _____

6. up / your reports / Write _____

7. in / them / Hand _____

8. off / Take / your lab coats _____

9. them / Put / away _____

10. the lab / Clean / up _____

6 EDITING

Read this student's journal notes. Find and correct nine mistakes in the use of phrasal verbs. The first mistake is already corrected.

Sept. 2

I just got ~~back~~ from Venezuela ~~back~~! I spent two weeks in the Amazon rain forest with Dr. Rodriguez's research group. We carried out research there on plants that the Piaroa people use as medicine. We made down a list of these plants, and we're going to analyze them when we get back to school next week.

We set down camp near the Orinoco River, hundreds of miles from any major city. Life there is hard. You get very early up every morning. You must always watch up and never touch a new insect or plant. If you pick up it, you can get a bad skin rash. But plants can also cure. One day, I felt sick. One of the Piaroa gave me the stem of a certain plant to chew. It worked! Later I found at that the same plant helps cure insect bites. And believe me, insects are a big problem in the rain forest. I used up many bottles of repellent. But even when I put on it, it didn't totally keep the insects away.

This trip changed my life! I'm now thinking about switching my major to pharmacology. I want to find over more about how people can use the same plants that animals use as medicine.

COMMUNICATION PRACTICE

7 LISTENING

Listen to these short conversations that take place in a college science lab. Circle the phrasal verbs that you hear. Then listen again and check your answers.

1. A: What's Terry doing?
   B: She's <u>handing in</u> / (handing out) some lab reports.

2. A: Are you done with your report, Rea?
   B: Almost. I just have to <u>look up / look over</u> some information.

3. A: Hey, guys. That music is disturbing us.
   B: Sorry. We'll <u>turn it down / turn it off</u>.

4. A: Jason is discouraged.
   B: I know. He says he can't <u>keep on / keep up</u> in class.

5. A: Did you hear about Lila?
   B: Yes, we were all surprised when she <u>dropped in / dropped out</u> yesterday.

6. A: OK, class. It's time to <u>take back / take off</u> your lab coats.
   B: Oh, could we have a few more minutes? We're almost done.

Now look at your completed sentences. Decide if the statements below are **True (T)** *or* **False (F)**.

___F___ **7.** Terry is giving some reports to the teacher.

_____ **8.** Rea is going to look for some information in a reference book.

_____ **9.** They're going to make the music lower.

_____ **10.** Jason feels that the class is going too fast for him.

_____ **11.** Lila visited the class yesterday.

_____ **12.** It's time to return the lab coats.

8 LET'S TALK IT OVER

Work in groups. Imagine that you are going to take a class field trip. Decide where to go—for example, the zoo, a museum, a park. Then assign tasks and make a To Do *list. Try to include some of these phrasal verbs.*

call up	clean up	drop off	empty out	figure out	hand out
look over	look up	make up	pass out	pick out	pick up
put away	set up	take back	talk over	turn on	write down

EXAMPLE:
A: I'll write down the To Do list.
B: Good idea. I'll call up to find out the hours.
C: I can pick up a bus schedule.

❾ A NEW LEAF

Discuss the pictures below with a partner. Who are the people, and what are they doing in each picture? Then make up a story about the pictures, and write a number under each picture to show the sequence. Then write your story. Compare your story to your classmates' stories. Talk over any differences. There is more than one way to tell a story!

> **EXAMPLE:**
> In this picture, three people are talking to a plant doctor . . .

a. _____   b. _____   c. _____

d. _____   e. _____   f. _____

❿ WRITING

Dr. Eloy Rodriguez is a role model to his students. Who was your most important role model when you were growing up? Why did you pick this person? What problems did your role model help you out with? What ideas and actions did you pick up from this person? Write a paragraph. Use phrasal verbs.

> **EXAMPLE:**
> When I was growing up, my role model was my high school chemistry teacher. I picked Ms. Suarez because she was a good teacher.
> She helped me out when I didn't understand the lesson, and she . . .

REVIEW OR SELFTEST

I. *Circle the correct pronouns to complete the article.*

When Marta's company laid (her) / herself off, she told her / herself it was time

_{1.}   _{2.}

to start her own business. Like Marta, a lot of people dream about starting

their / one another's own businesses and working for them / themselves.

_{3.}   _{4.}

Unfortunately, very few succeed. Are you a self-starter? Read about the

qualities of successful business owners and decide for you / yourself.

                                                _{5.}

- Do you have a lot of energy? Self-starters have lots of energy. They push

  itself / themselves very hard, and their families often have to force

  _{6.}

  them / itself to take a break.

  _{7.}

- How well do you work in groups? Good team members work well with

  each other / themselves, but a self-starter must lead them / themselves.

  _{8.}   _{9.}

- Do you like to challenge you / yourself? Self-starters get bored when things

                                          _{10.}

  are too easy.

- Are you self-confident? Self-starters have lots of self-confidence. You need to

  believe in herself / yourself even when nobody else believes in

                                  _{11.}

  you / yourself.

  _{12.}

- Do you have social support? Self-starters need good friends and family, so

  don't forget themselves / them when you get busy. Even independent people

                                    _{13.}

  listen to each other's / his problems.

                      _{14.}

II. *Complete the article. Choose the phrasal verb from the box that is closest in meaning to the words in parentheses. Use the correct form of the phrasal verb.*

find out	get back	get by	go on	~~grow up~~	hand over
help out	look up	pass over	pick out	set up	turn into

When you were ___growing up___ , did you think that tomatoes grew in supermarkets?

1. (becoming an adult)

Did you realize that cotton was a plant before it _____ your new gym

2. (changed into)

socks? New Yorker Wendy Dubit _____ that a lot of city kids don't

3. (learned)

know anything about farms. She used her own money to _____

4. (establish)

Farm Hands/City Hands. This organization buses city people to small farms.

Children and adults from all social classes _____ on family farms and

5. (assist)

receive room and food in exchange. They also learn things you can't _____.

6. (try to find in a book)

One lawyer noted, "I worked with the tomatoes for weeks. Now I can

_____ the perfectly ripe ones and _____ the ones that

7. (select) 8. (decide not to use)

need a few more days on the vine." Many people start small gardens of their own

when they _____ to the city.

9. (return)

After the success of Farm Hands/City Hands, Dubit _____ to invent

10. (continued)

Project Ongoing to train homeless people in farm work and food services. The project has

been so successful that participants _____ on the food that they grow. They

11. (survive)

sell any extra. They _____ the profits _____ to the program.

12. (give)

III. *Complete each conversation with a phrasal verb and a pronoun.*

1. A: This field trip will be difficult. Please think over your decision carefully.

   B: OK. I'll ___think it over___ this weekend and let you know on Monday.

2. A: Did you write down the flight number for our trip?

   B: Yes, I _____ on an envelope. Now where did I put the envelope?

3. A: Are we going to pick up Pam on the way to the airport?

   B: No. We don't have to _____. She has a ride.

(continued on next page)

4. A: Don't forget to put on your hat. That sun is hot.

    B: I'll _____ before I leave.

5. A: Someone please help out Ramón. That pack's too heavy for one person.

    B: OK. I'll _____. We can carry it together.

6. A: Let's set up our camp near the lake.

    B: Too many mosquitoes there. Let's _____ on the hill.

7. A: Why did you pick out cat's claw to study? It's such a common plant.

    B: I _____ because people use it for a lot of different things.

8. A: When are you going to write up your notes?

    B: I'll _____ as soon as we get back.

IV. *Circle the letter of the correct answer to complete each sentence.*

1. Maria often goes to the movies by _____.   A B C **(D)**
  (A) themselves   (C) alone
  (B) her   (D) herself

2. Paul set _____ his own business in 1999.   A B C D
  (A) out   (C) down
  (B) up   (D) at

3. That frog is poisonous. Don't _____!   A B C D
  (A) pick it up   (C) pick up
  (B) pick up it   (D) pick it

4. Sharon didn't want to study, but she talked _____ into it.   A B C D
  (A) each other   (C) them
  (B) himself   (D) herself

5. We're going your way. Do you want us to _____ at home?   A B C D
  (A) drop you off   (C) drop you down
  (B) dropping you off   (D) drop off you

6. When Brad and I study together, we help _____ a lot.   A B C D
  (A) us   (C) each other
  (B) them   (D) her

7. After Toni graduated from high school, she went _____ to   **A B C D**
college.
   (A) over   (C) on
   (B) herself   (D) himself

8. Pat borrowed three books from me, and he hasn't given   **A B C D**
_____ yet.
   (A) them back   (C) back them
   (B) it back   (D) back it

9. Please put _____ your lab coats before you leave the   **A B C D**
laboratory.
   (A) off   (C) up
   (B) away   (D) in

10. Could you turn _____ the music so we can sleep?   **A B C D**
   (A) down   (C) over
   (B) away   (D) up

11. We'll turn _____ and go to sleep, too.   **A B C D**
   (A) it off   (C) it away
   (B) off it   (D) away it

V. *Read this student's essay. Find and correct eight mistakes in the use of pronouns and phrasal verbs. The first mistake is already corrected.*

I have three older brothers, but my role model is my next oldest brother,
                           me
Orlando. Orlando was always there for ~~myself~~ when we were growing up. I was
very small, and he always kept the bullies away. When I couldn't figure up
homework problems by myself, he helped out me. Orlando never gave up when he
had problems. Once in high school, my baseball team passed myself up for
pitcher. I wanted to quit the team, but he talked me over playing. In fact, he
woke early every morning up to practice with me. When they chose me for pitcher
the following year, we were really proud of ourselves—he was proud of me for
succeeding, and I was proud of himself for being such a great coach.

▶ *To check your answers, go to the Answer Key on page 111.*

FROM GRAMMAR TO WRITING
USING PRONOUNS FOR COHERENCE

When you write a paragraph, it is usually better to use pronouns than to repeat the same noun. Pronouns can make your writing smoother and more connected.

> **EXAMPLE:**
> My apartment is pretty comfortable. I hope you enjoy staying in my apartment. ⟶
>
> My apartment is pretty comfortable. I hope you enjoy staying in **it**.

1 *Read this note from Ted, thanking Felicia in advance for housesitting. Circle all the pronouns. Above each pronoun, write the noun that it refers to.*

Dear Felicia,

Thanks for staying in my apartment next weekend and taking care of the dog. Help Felicia yourself to the food in the fridge—you can use it all up if you like. I rented some videos for you. They're on top of the TV. I picked out some action movies. I hope you like them. The VCR is easy to use, but remember to turn it down at 11:00 P.M. My upstairs neighbor is very touchy about noise. There are just a few other things to remember. Red's friendly, but please keep her away from my neighbor's poodle. They don't like each other. Her bowl is on the kitchen counter. Fill it up once a day with dry food. Please walk her twice a day. When you go out, remember to turn on the answering machine. It's in the living room. The Sunday newspaper arrives at about 8:00 A.M. Pick it up early—sometimes it disappears! When you leave for work Monday, just leave the keys with Mrs. Delgado next door. I'll get them from her when I get back.

Thanks again!

Ted

2 *Read this note. Change the nouns to pronouns when you can. With phrasal verbs, remember to put the pronoun between the main verb and the particle.*

Dear Dara,

Welcome! I hope you enjoy staying here this week. Here are a few things to keep in mind: The mail is delivered every day around noon. You'll find
it
the ~~mail~~ in the mailbox in front of the building. Please pick up the mail and put the mail on the dining room table. Feel free to use the air conditioner, but please turn off the air conditioner when you leave the house. There's plenty of food in the refrigerator! Please feel free to use up the food. I'm expecting a few phone calls. If you're home, could you please take a message? Just write down the message on the yellow pad in the top left desk drawer. I think the apartment is pretty comfortable. I hope you enjoy staying in the apartment. Make yourself at home!

See you in a week.

Rachel

3 *Before you write . . .*

- Imagine that a friend is going to take care of your home while you are away. What will your friend's responsibilities be? What special things do you need to tell him or her about your home or neighborhood? Make a list.

- Exchange lists with a partner. Ask questions about your partner's list. Answer your partner's questions.

   EXAMPLE:
   A: How often should I take out the garbage?
   B: Oh, you can take it out every other day. Where do you keep the dog food?

4 *Write a note to your friend on another piece of paper. Give instructions about taking care of your home. Include answers to your partner's questions in Exercise 3. Use pronouns and phrasal verbs.*

5 *Exchange notes with a different partner. Complete the chart.*

a. Did the writer use pronouns where necessary?   Yes _____ No _____

b. Put a question mark (?) over each pronoun you think is in the wrong place.

c. Complete this chart of daily tasks. If you have a question, ask your partner, and write the answer on the chart.

EXAMPLES:
Sunday: water the plants, feed the pets, pick up the newspaper
Monday: feed the pets, pick up the mail and put it on the hall table

Day	Tasks

Rewrite your note. Make any necessary changes in your use of pronouns. Add information that your partner requested.

REVIEW OR SELFTEST
ANSWER KEY

I. (Unit 9)

2. herself
3. their
4. themselves
5. yourself
6. themselves
7. them
8. each other
9. them
10. yourself
11. yourself
12. you
13. them
14. each other's

II. (Unit 10)

2. turned into
3. found out
4. set up
5. help out
6. look up
7. pick out
8. pass over
9. get back
10. went on
11. get by
12. hand . . . over

III. (Unit 10)

2. wrote it down
3. pick her up
4. put it on
5. help him out
6. set it up
7. picked it out
8. write them up

IV. (Units 9 and 10)

2. B
3. A
4. D
5. A
6. C
7. C
8. A
9. B
10. A
11. A

V. (Units 9 and 10)

I have three older brothers, but my role model is my next oldest brother, Orlando. Orlando was always there for ~~myself~~ [me] when we were growing up. I was very small, and he always kept the bullies away. When I couldn't figure ~~up~~ [out] homework problems by myself, he helped ~~out me~~ [me out]. Orlando never gave up when he had problems. Once, in high school, my baseball team passed ~~myself~~ [me] up for pitcher. I wanted to quit the team, but he talked me ~~over~~ [into] playing. In fact, he woke[up]^ early every morning ~~up~~ to practice with me. When they chose me for pitcher the following year, we were really proud of ~~ourselves~~ [each other]—he was proud of me for succeeding, and I was proud of ~~himself~~ [him] for being such a great coach.

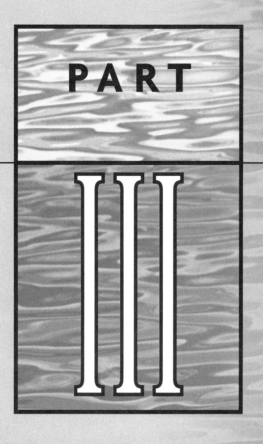

PART

III

MODALS
AND
RELATED VERBS
AND EXPRESSIONS

ABILITY:
CAN, COULD, BE ABLE TO

GRAMMAR IN CONTEXT

BEFORE YOU READ What are the people in the photograph doing? Look at the title of the article. Guess the main point.

Read this newspaper article.

Born to Dance
by V. Gupta

"Who made up the rule that you **can** only **dance** on your two feet . . . ?" asks Mary Verdi-Fletcher, president and founding director of Cleveland Ballet Dancing Wheels. She is also one of its main dancers. Verdi-Fletcher was born with a medical condition that affects the nervous system. By the age of twelve, she **was not able to stand** or **walk**. That didn't stop her from dancing. People said, "You **can't walk**; how **can** you **be** a dancer?" Verdi-Fletcher, however, *knew* it was possible to dance in her wheelchair because, as she says, "Dance is an emotion that comes from within."

When she entered her first dance competition, the audience was confused. "She's in a wheelchair. How **can** she **dance**?" But at the end of the performance, they stood and applauded. Not only **could** she **dance**, but she **could hypnotize** an audience with her talent. When the artistic director of the Cleveland Ballet first saw her, he thought, "*That* is a dancer. . . . You **can't take** your eyes off her."

Dancing Wheels has both "sitdown dancers" and "standup dancers." The group offers a new definition of dance. It also changes the perception of what people **can** or **cannot do**. "Through our dance," says Verdi-Fletcher, "we want to show that anything is possible and achievable. . . . People need to see they **can achieve** their dreams and aspirations—but not without a lot of hard work and dedication."

GRAMMAR **PRESENTATION**
ABILITY: *CAN AND COULD*

STATEMENTS			
SUBJECT	**CAN / COULD* (NOT)**	**BASE FORM OF VERB**	
I You He She We You They	**can (not)**	**dance**	now.
	could (not)		last year.

CONTRACTIONS		
cannot OR can not	=	**can't**
could not	=	**couldn't**

*Can and *could* are modals. Modals have only one form. They do not have *-s* in the third-person singular.

YES / NO QUESTIONS		
CAN / COULD	**SUBJECT**	**BASE FORM OF VERB**
Can	I you he she we you they	**dance?**
Could		

SHORT ANSWERS		
AFFIRMATIVE		
Yes,	you I he she	**can.**
	you we they	**could.**

SHORT ANSWERS		
NEGATIVE		
No,	you I he she	**can't.**
	you we they	**couldn't.**

WH- QUESTIONS			
WH- WORD	**CAN / COULD**	**SUBJECT**	**BASE FORM OF VERB**
How well	**can** **could**	she you	**dance?**

(continued on next page)

ABILITY: *BE ABLE TO*

STATEMENTS			
SUBJECT	BE	(NOT) ABLE TO	BASE FORM OF VERB
I	**am**		
You	**are**		
He She	**is**	**(not) able to**	**practice**.
We You They	**are**		

YES / NO QUESTIONS			
BE	SUBJECT	ABLE TO	BASE FORM OF VERB
Is	she	**able to**	**practice**?
Are	you		

SHORT ANSWERS		
AFFIRMATIVE		
Yes,	she	**is**.
	I	**am**.

SHORT ANSWERS		
NEGATIVE		
No,	she	**isn't**.
	I'm	**not**.

WH- QUESTIONS				
WH- WORD	BE	SUBJECT	ABLE TO	BASE FORM OF VERB
When	**is**	she	**able to**	**practice**?
How often	**are**	you		

NOTES

EXAMPLES

1. Use *can* to describe an <u>ability in the present</u>.

- She **can dance**, but she **can't skate**.
- **Can** she **swim**?

2. You can also use *be able to* to describe an <u>ability in the present or future</u>.

USAGE NOTE: In everyday speech, *can* is much <u>more common</u> than *be able to* in the <u>present</u> tense.

- The new student **is able to park** a car, but she**'s not able to drive** in traffic yet.
- They**'ll be able to get** tickets for Friday's dance performance, but they **won't be able to get** front-row seats.
- I **can park** a car, but I **can't drive** in traffic yet.

3. Use either *could* or *was / were able to* to describe a <u>general ability in the past</u>.

- Mary **could drive** a car with special hand controls.

  OR

- Mary **was able to drive** a car with special hand controls.

4. You must use *was / were able to* to describe a <u>special achievement</u> or a <u>single event in the past</u>.

- In 1979, they **were able to win** second prize in a dance competition.
  Not ~~In 1979, they could win second prize in a dance competition.~~

5. You can use either *couldn't* or *wasn't / weren't able to* for any negative sentence <u>describing past ability</u>—either general or specific.

GENERAL ABILITY
- She **couldn't walk**.

  OR

- She **wasn't able to walk**.

SPECIAL ACHIEVEMENT
- They **couldn't win** their first competition.

  OR

- They **weren't able to win** their first competition.

6. For forms and tenses <u>other than the present or past</u>, you must use *be able to*.

- Al wants **to be able to take** dance lessons next year. *(infinitive form)*
- By June he**'ll be able to dance** at his wedding. *(future)*

REFERENCE NOTE
Can and *could* are also used to ask and give permission *(see Unit 12)*, make requests *(see Unit 13)*, and make assumptions *(see Unit 36)*.
Could is also used to make suggestions *(see Unit 15)* and express future possibility *(see Unit 35)*.

FOCUSED PRACTICE

1 DISCOVER THE GRAMMAR

Look at this information about Mary Verdi-Fletcher. Then decide whether the statements below are **True (T)** *or* **False (F)**. *Put a question mark* **(?)** *if there isn't enough information.*

Mary Verdi-Fletcher	
1955	born in Ohio
1975	graduated from high school
	got job as keypunch operator
1978	learned to drive
1979	entered Dance Fever Competition
1980	began Dancing Wheels
	enrolled in Lakeland Community College, Ohio
	took course in public speaking
1980–1988	worked for Independent Living Center
1984	married Robert Fletcher
1989–90	tour director for Cleveland Ballet
1990–present	founding director and dancer, Cleveland Ballet Dancing Wheels
	teaches dance to people with and without disabilities
Awards:	Outstanding Young Clevelander Award (1990)
	Oracle Merit Award (1991)
	Invacare Award of Excellence in the Arts (1994)
	Governor's Award for Outreach (1998)
Other Interests:	watching football and soccer games

___T__ **1.** Mary was able to get a job after high school.

_____ **2.** She can't drive a car.

_____ **3.** She couldn't participate in dance competitions.

_____ **4.** She can speak foreign languages.

_____ **5.** She was able to start a dance company.

_____ **6.** She couldn't finish college.

_____ **7.** She can probably speak well in front of large groups of people.

_____ **8.** She'll be able to help people with disabilities learn to dance.

_____ **9.** She can play the piano.

2 NOW I CAN Grammar Notes 1, 3, and 5

Complete the paragraphs with **can, can't, could,** *or* **couldn't.**

1. For a long time, Jim and Marie _____couldn't_____ agree on a family sport. Jim
   _{a.}

   loves tennis, and Marie takes lessons, but she still _____ play. Marie
   _{b.}

   _____ swim, but Jim hates the water. They recently took up dancing.
   _{c.}

   Soon, they _____ tango beautifully together.
   _{d.}

2. Stefan has made a lot of progress in English. Last semester he _____
a.

order a meal in a restaurant or talk on the telephone. His friends helped him do

everything. Now he _____ speak English in a lot of situations.
b.

3. Bill almost _____ make his class presentation last semester because he
a.

was so nervous. He _____ communicate well in small groups, but not in
b.

big ones. He plans to take a course in public speaking soon. I'm sure he

_____ improve quickly.
c.

4. Last year I _____ dance at all, but when I met Stan, I signed up for a
a.

class right away. He _____ really dance, and I wanted to dance with him.
b.

Now I _____ do the basic steps. I _____ do the waltz yet, but
c.   d.

we're planning to waltz at our wedding next month.

❸ AT THE DANCE STUDIO

Complete each conversation with the correct form of **be able to** *and the verb in parentheses.*

1. A: I heard your sister wanted to take lessons. _____Was_____ she __able to start__ ?
a. (start)

B: Yes, she was. She started last month. She can do the fox-trot now, but she still

_____ the waltz.
b. (do)

2. A: Why are you taking dance lessons?

B: I want to _____ at my wedding!
a. (dance)

3. A: _____ you _____ Russian as a child, Mrs. Suraikin?
a. (speak)

B: Yes, I was. We spoke it at home, so I _____ it fluently.
b. (speak)

A: _____ your children _____ Russian, too?
c. (speak)

B: No, unfortunately my children never learned Russian. They only speak English.

4. A: I _____ last weekend. I hurt my ankle.
a. (not practice)

B: That's too bad. _____ you _____ next week?
b. (practice)

A: I hope so. I'll call you on Monday. Maybe we _____ on Tuesday.
c. (get together)

4 ACHIEVEMENT

*Complete the advertisement. Use the appropriate form of **can**, **could**, or **be able to** with each verb. Use **can** or **could** when possible.*

WILL B. HAPPY®
Professional Development Courses

Time Management   Presentations   Career Development   Teamwork

Think about your last presentation: ____Were____ you ____able to prepare____ on time?
                                                          1. (prepare)

_____ you _____ your ideas?
                              2. (communicate)

***Will B. Happy*®** has helped others, and he _____ YOU!
                                                            3. (help)

"Before I took Will B. Happy's course, my work was always late because

I _____ a schedule. I also had big piles on my desk because I
        4. (follow)

_____ what was important. Now I _____ my time
        5. (decide)   6. (manage)

effectively. Next month, when my workload gets heavy, I _____ it and
                                                                      7. (organize)

do the important things first."

—*Scott Mathis, student*

"I didn't use to _____ in front of groups. Now I can!"
                      8. (speak)

—*Mary Zhang, sales manager*

---

5 EDITING

Read this student's journal. Find and correct seven mistakes in the use of modals.
The first mistake is already corrected.

◯	Today in my Will. B. Happy Teamwork course, I learned about work styles—"Drivers" and
	"Enthusiasts." I'm a Driver, so I can make decisions, but I'm not able ^to^ listen to other
	people's ideas. The Enthusiast in our group can communicates well, but you can't
	depend on her. Now I understand what was happening in my business class last year,
	when I couldn't felt comfortable with my team. I thought that they all talked too much
	and didn't able to work efficiently. I could get an A for the course, but it was hard. I
	can do a lot more alone, but some jobs are too big for that. Our instructor says that
	soon Drivers will able to listen, and the Enthusiasts could be more dependable.

COMMUNICATION PRACTICE

6 LISTENING

Karl is interviewing for the job of office manager at Carmen's Dance Studio. Listen to the conversation. Then listen again and check all the things that Karl can do now.

☑ answer the phones ☐ design a monthly newsletter
☐ speak another language ☐ schedule appointments
☐ use a computer ☐ drive
☐ type 50 words per minute ☐ dance

7 INFORMATION GAP: CAN THEY DO THE TANGO?

Students at Carmen's Dance Studio are preparing for a dance recital in June. It is now the end of April. Can students do all the dances featured in the recital by now?

Work in pairs (A and B). Student B, look at the Information Gap on page 123 and follow the instructions there. Student A, ask your partner for the information you need to complete the schedule. Answer your partner's questions.

EXAMPLE:

A: Can your students do the Argentine tango?

B: No, they can't. But they'll be able to do it by the end of May. Can they do the cha-cha?

A: Yes, they can. They could do it in March.

CARMEN'S DANCE STUDIO
Schedule of Dance Classes

Dances	March	April	May
Argentine Tango			✓
Cha-Cha	✓		
Fox-Trot			
Hustle			✓
Mambo			
Merengue	✓		
Salsa			✓
Swing			
Tango		✓	
Waltz			

When you are finished, compare schedules. Are they the same?

8 CLASS PRESENTATION

Work in a small group. Imagine you are planning a class presentation. Look at the list of skills and tell each other what you **can** *and* **can't** *do. Add to the list. Then assign tasks to the group members.*

do library research

do research online

type on a computer

make charts and graphs

photocopy handouts

take photographs

interview people

make the presentation

_____

_____

EXAMPLE:

A: Can you do library research?

B: Yes, but I can't do research online yet.

9 WRITING

Write one or two paragraphs about a person who has succeeded in spite of some kind of difficulty or problem. You can choose a famous person whom you have never met or anyone you know. Use **can**, **could**, *and* **be able to**.

Student B, answer your partner's questions. Ask your partner for the information you need to complete the schedule.

EXAMPLE:

A: Can your students do the Argentine tango?

B: No, they can't. But they'll be able to do it by the end of May. Can they do the cha-cha?

A: Yes, they can. They could do it in March.

CARMEN'S DANCE STUDIO
Schedule of Dance Classes

Dances	March	April	May
Argentine Tango			✓
Cha-Cha	✓		
Fox-Trot		✓	
Hustle			
Mambo		✓	
Merengue			
Salsa			
Swing	✓		
Tango			
Waltz	✓		

When you are finished, compare schedules. Are they the same?

PERMISSION:
MAY, COULD, CAN,
DO YOU MIND IF . . . ?

GRAMMAR **IN CONTEXT**

BEFORE YOU READ What do you know about the TOEFL® test? What's your opinion about this test?

▭ *Read this excerpt from a booklet about the Test of English as a Foreign Language (TOEFL®).*

SOME FREQUENTLY ASKED QUESTIONS ABOUT THE TOEFL® TEST

Q: **Can I take** the TOEFL test more than once?

A: Yes. **You can take** the TOEFL test as many times as you want, but **you may** only **take** it one time per calendar month.

Q: **May I register** for the test on the same day as the test?

A: No, **you may not.** You must register before the test.

Q: I'm a doctor. **Could I wear** my beeper during the test?

A: Sorry, but no cell phones, beepers, pagers, or watch alarms are permitted.

Q: My students are going to take the test for the first time. They don't want schools to see bad test scores. **Can they cancel** their scores after the test?

A: Immediately following the test, **they may choose** to see their scores on the screen OR **they may cancel** them. Once they see their scores, **they cannot cancel** them. However, **they may** always **choose** not to send them to any schools.

Structure
Directions: Click on the one word or phrase that best completes the sentence.

How many times may a student _____ the TOEFL?

- ● take
- ○ takes
- ○ to take
- ○ taking

TIME	HELP	Confirm Answer	NEXT

GRAMMAR **PRESENTATION**

PERMISSION: *MAY, COULD, CAN, DO YOU MIND IF . . . ?*

QUESTIONS: *MAY / COULD / CAN*

MAY / COULD / CAN*	**SUBJECT**	**BASE FORM OF VERB**	
May **Could** **Can**	I he she we they	**start**	now?

**May, could,* and *can* are modals. Modals have only one form. They do not have *-s* in the third-person singular.

SHORT ANSWERS

AFFIRMATIVE

Yes,	you he she they	**may**. **can**.

Sure.
Certainly.
Of course.
Why not?

SHORT ANSWERS

NEGATIVE

No,	you he she they	**may not**. **can't**.

NOTE: *May not* is not contracted.

QUESTIONS: *DO YOU MIND IF . . . ?*

DO YOU MIND IF	**SUBJECT**	**VERB**
Do you mind if	I we they	**start**?
	he she it	**starts**?

SHORT ANSWERS

AFFIRMATIVE

Not at all.
No, I **don't**.
Go right ahead.

SHORT ANSWERS

NEGATIVE

Yes, I **do**.

STATEMENTS: *MAY / CAN*

SUBJECT	*MAY / CAN (NOT)*	**BASE FORM OF VERB**	
You He They	**may (not)** **can (not)**	**start**	now.

NOTES	EXAMPLES
1. Use *may, could* and *can* to <u>ask permission</u>.	• **May** I **call** you next Friday? • **Could** we **use** our dictionaries? • **Can** he **come** to class with me next week?
USAGE NOTE: Some people feel that *may* is more formal than *can* and *could*. You can use *may* when you ask <u>formal permission</u> to do something.	• **May** I **leave** the room, Professor Lee?
▶ **BE CAREFUL!** Requests for permission always <u>refer to the present or the future</u>. When you use *could* to ask for permission, it is not past tense.	**A:** **Could** I register for the test *tomorrow*? **B:** Certainly. The office will be open at 9:00 A.M.

2. We often say *please* when we ask permission. Note the word order.	• **Could** I ask a question, *please*? • **May** I *please* ask a question?

3. Use *Do you mind if . . . ?* to ask for permission when it is possible your action will inconvenience someone or make someone uncomfortable.	**A:** **Do you mind if** I clean up tomorrow? **B:** Yes, actually, I do mind. I hate to see a mess in the kitchen in the morning.
▶ **BE CAREFUL!** A <u>negative answer</u> to the question *Do you mind if . . . ?* gives permission to do something. It means "It's OK. I don't mind."	**A:** **Do you mind if** my brother comes to class with me? **B:** *Not at all.* *(Your brother may come with you.)*

4. Use *may* or *can* to <u>answer requests for permission</u>. Don't use *could* in answers.

A: **Could** I borrow this pencil?
B: Yes, of course you **can**.
Not ~~Yes, you could.~~
~~No, you couldn't.~~

▶ **BE CAREFUL!** Do not contract *may not*.

• No, you **may not**.
Not ~~No, you mayn't.~~

We also frequently use certain **expressions** instead of modals to <u>answer requests for permission</u>.

A: **Could** I close the window?
B: *Sure.*
Certainly.
Go ahead.
No, please don't. It's hot in here.

---

5. When people **refuse permission**, they usually do so indirectly. They soften the refusal <u>with an apology and an explanation</u>.

Sometimes, when the <u>rules are very clear</u>, someone will refuse permission without an apology or an explanation.

STUDENT: Can I please have five more minutes to answer this question?
TEACHER: *I'm sorry, but the time is up.*

DRIVER: Can I park here?
OFFICER: *No, you can't.*

REFERENCE NOTE
May, *can,* and *could* are also used to express possibility. *(See Unit 35.)*
Can and *could* are also used to talk about ability and to make requests. *(See Units 11 and 13.)*

FOCUSED PRACTICE

1 DISCOVER THE GRAMMAR

Write the letter of the correct response to each request for permission.

a. No, he can't. He has to complete an accident report first.

b. Not at all. There's plenty of time.

c. Sure they can. There's plenty of room.

d. Yes, you may. The test starts in ten minutes.

e. I'm sorry, he's not in. Can I take a message?

f. Certainly. Here they are.

1. ___d___

2. _____

3. _____

4. _____

5. _____

6. _____

2 GIVING THE GO-AHEAD

Mr. Hamad is supervising a test. Complete each conversation with the word in parentheses and the correct pronouns.

1. (can)

MR. HAMAD: It's 9:00. _____You can_____ come into the room now. Please show me
   a.
your registration forms as you come in.

SOFIA: My brother isn't taking the test. _____ come in with me?
   b.

MR. HAMAD: No, I'm sorry, _____. Only people with tickets are permitted
   c. (negative)
in the exam room.

2. (may)

MR. HAMAD: I'm going to hand out the tests now. Write your name on the front in
pencil, but don't start the test yet. Remember, _____ start
   a. (negative)
the test until I tell you to.

AHMED: I'm sorry I'm late. _____ come in?
   b.

MR. HAMAD: Yes, _____. We haven't started the test yet.
   c.

3. (could)

ROSA: _____ use a pen to write my name?
   a.

MR. HAMAD: No, you have to use a pencil.

ROSA: Jamie, _____ borrow this pencil, please? I only
   b.
brought a pen.

JAMIE: Sure, take it. I brought a few.

4. (can)

MR. HAMAD: OK. We're ready to start. Open your test booklets and read the
instructions.

JEAN: Excuse me. We're late because our train broke down. _____
   a.
still come in?

MR. HAMAD: I'm sorry, _____. We've already started the test.
   b. (negative)

3 TAKING THE TEST

Read the directions to this section of a test similar to part of the TOEFL®.
Then complete the test questions.

Directions: These conversations take place on a train. Each conversation has four underlined words or phrases. They are marked (A), (B), (C), and (D). Find the underlined word or phrase that is incorrect. Fill in the space that corresponds to the letter of the incorrect word or phrase.

Example

    <u>May</u> we <u>board</u> the train yet?
     A   B
    <u>No</u>, you <u>mayn't</u> board until 12:30.
     C   D

Sample Answer

Ⓐ Ⓑ Ⓒ ⬤

1.   <u>Can</u> he <u>comes</u> on the train with me?
      A   B
    I'm <u>sorry</u>, but only passengers <u>can</u> board the train.
        C   D

Ⓐ Ⓑ Ⓒ Ⓓ

2.   <u>Do</u> you <u>mind</u> if I sit <u>here</u>?
     A   B   C
    <u>No, I don't</u>. This seat is taken.
       D

Ⓐ Ⓑ Ⓒ Ⓓ

3.   <u>Could</u> I <u>looked</u> at your newspaper?
       A   B
    <u>Yes</u>, of course you <u>can</u>.
     C   D

Ⓐ Ⓑ Ⓒ Ⓓ

4.   <u>Can</u> I <u>to get</u> through, <u>please</u>?
     A   B   C
    Yes, <u>of course</u>. I'll move my bag.
        D

Ⓐ Ⓑ Ⓒ Ⓓ

5.   <u>Could</u> we <u>change</u> seats? I'd like to sit next
      A   B
    to my daughter.

    <u>Yes</u>, <u>we could</u>. No problem.
     C   D

Ⓐ Ⓑ Ⓒ Ⓓ

6.   Do you mind if <u>she</u> <u>play</u> her computer game?
         A   B C
    It's a little noisy.

    <u>No</u>, not at all.
     D

Ⓐ Ⓑ Ⓒ Ⓓ

7.   Can <u>we'll</u> get a sandwich soon, <u>please</u>?
        A   B
    I'm hungry.

    <u>Sure</u> we <u>can</u>. Let's go find the club car.
     C   D

Ⓐ Ⓑ Ⓒ Ⓓ

4 CELEBRATING

Lucy got high TOEFL® scores. She's going to celebrate by attending a concert with some friends. Write questions to ask for permission. Use the words in parentheses.

1. Lucy's friend Carl came to pick her up for the concert. He wants his friend Bob to come along.

   CARL: I have an extra ticket. <u>Do you mind if Bob comes along?</u>
   (Do you mind if)

   LUCY: Not at all.

2. Carl decides to call Bob and invite him. He wants to use Lucy's phone.

   CARL: Great. I'll call him right now. _____
   (Could)

   LUCY: Sure. It's in the kitchen.

3. Carl, Bob, and Lucy want to park in front of the stadium. Lucy asks a police officer.

   LUCY: Excuse me, officer. We're going to the concert.

   _____
   (Can)

   OFFICER: No, you can't. It's a tow-away zone.

4. The usher at the concert wants to see their tickets.

   USHER: _____
   (May / please)

   CARL: Certainly. Here they are.

5. Lucy, Bob, and Carl want to move up a few rows. Bob asks an usher.

   BOB: All those seats are empty. _____
   (Could / please)

   USHER: Sure. Go right ahead.

6. Bob and Carl want to tape the concert. Lucy asks the usher first.

   LUCY: My friends brought their tape recorder.

   _____
   (Can)

   USHER: No, they can't. No one is allowed to record the concert or take pictures.

7. Lucy hates the music, and she wants to leave. Bob and Carl don't seem to like it either.

   LUCY: This music is giving me a headache.

   _____
   (Do you mind if)

   BOB: I don't mind.

   CARL: Me neither. Let's *all* leave.

COMMUNICATION PRACTICE

5 LISTENING

Listen and write the number of each conversation. Then listen again and decide if permission was given or refused. Check the appropriate column.

	permission given	permission refused
_____ **a.** child / parent	☐	☐
_____ **b.** travel agent / customer	☐	☐
__1__ **c.** police officer / driver	☑	☐
_____ **d.** boyfriend / girlfriend's mother	☐	☐
_____ **e.** employee / employer	☐	☐

6 ASKING PERMISSION

Work in small groups. Read the following situations and decide what to say. Think of as many things to say as possible.

1. You're visiting some good friends. The weather is very cold, but they don't seem to mind. Their windows are open, and the heat is off. You're freezing.

   > **EXAMPLES:**
   > Do you mind if I close the windows?
   > May I borrow that sweater?
   > Can I turn on the heat?
   > Could I make some hot tea?

2. Your teacher is explaining something to the class, and you're getting completely confused. The teacher is very friendly, and he has office hours several times a week. He also spends a lot of time talking to students after class.

3. You have a small apartment. Two friends are coming to visit your town for a week, and they want to stay with you. What can you say to your roommate?

4. You're at a concert with some friends. You like the performer very much. You have your tape recorder and your camera with you. Sometimes this performer talks to fans and signs programs after the concert.

5. You have formed a TOEFL® study group with some classmates. You want to use a classroom on Thursday evenings to study. You would like to use your school's large cassette player for listening practice. Some of your classmates come directly from work. They would like permission to eat a sandwich in the classroom. Write a note to your teacher and ask for permission.

7 ROLE PLAY

Work in pairs. Read the following situations. Take turns being Student A and Student B.

Student A

1. You were absent from class yesterday. B, your classmate, always takes good notes.

Student B

1. A is in your class. You are always willing to help your classmates.

EXAMPLE:

A: May I copy your notes from class yesterday?

B: Sure. Here they are.

A: And could you tell me the assignment?

B: It's pages 20 through 25 in the textbook.

2. You're at work. You have a terrible headache. B is your boss.

3. You're a teenager. You and your friend want to travel to another city to see a concert. You want to borrow your family's car. Your friend has a license and wants to drive.

4. B has invited you to a small party. At the last minute, your two cousins show up. They have nothing to do the night of the party.

2. A is your employee. You have a lot of work for A to do today.

3. A is your son / daughter. You like this friend, and you have no objection to lending him or her the car. However, you want the friend to be careful.

4. Your party is at a restaurant, and you have already arranged for a certain number of people to attend. Besides, this is supposed to be a small party for a few of your close friends.

8 WRITING

Write two short notes asking permission. Choose situations from Exercise 7, or use situations of your own.

REQUESTS:
WILL, WOULD, COULD, CAN, WOULD YOU MIND . . . ?

GRAMMAR **IN CONTEXT**

BEFORE YOU READ What is Marcia's e-mail address? Who did Marcia send e-mail to?

 Read Marcia Jones's e-mail messages.

From: John Sanchez@dataline.com
To: Marciajones@dataline.com
Marcia:
I'll be out of town until Thursday. **Would** you please **photocopy** the monthly sales report for me? Thanks a lot!
John

From: MarciaJones@dataline.com
To: AnnChen@dataline.com
Hi, Ann—
I'm sending you a copy of our sales report. **Could** you **make** 25 copies? And **would you mind delivering** them to me when you're finished? It's a rush!
Thanks.
Marcia

From: RheaJones@island.net
To: MarciaJones@dataline.com
Marcia, dear—
Can you **drive** me to the Burtons after work today? They've invited me for dinner. Oh, and **will** you **pick up** something special at the bakery before you come? I told them I'd bring dessert.
Thanks, honey. —Mom

From: MarciaJones@dataline.com
To: RheaJones@island.net
Mom,
I'm sorry, but tonight I **can't**. I have to work late. Should I ask your favorite son-in-law if he can drive you? Let me know.
M.

GRAMMAR **PRESENTATION**

REQUESTS: *WILL, WOULD, COULD, CAN, WOULD YOU MIND . . . ?*

QUESTIONS: *WILL / WOULD / COULD / CAN*			
WILL / WOULD COULD / CAN*	SUBJECT	BASE FORM OF VERB	
Will **Would** **Could** **Can**	you	**mail**	this letter for me?
		drive	me to the doctor?
		pick up	some groceries?

*Will, would, could, and can are modals. Modals do not have -s in the third-person singular.

SHORT ANSWERS	
AFFIRMATIVE	
Sure Certainly Of course	(I **will**). (I **can**).

SHORT ANSWERS
NEGATIVE
I'm sorry, but I **can't**.

QUESTIONS: *WOULD YOU MIND . . . ?*		
WOULD YOU MIND	GERUND	
Would you mind	**mailing**	this letter for me?
	driving	me to the doctor?
	picking up	some groceries?

SHORT ANSWERS
AFFIRMATIVE
No, not at all. I'd be glad to.

SHORT ANSWERS
NEGATIVE
I'm sorry, but I can't.

NOTES	**EXAMPLES**

1. Use *will*, *would*, *could*, and *can* to <u>ask someone to do something</u>.

We often use *will* and *can* for <u>informal requests</u>.

We use *would* and *could* to <u>soften requests</u> and make them sound less demanding.

SISTER: **Will** you **bring** dessert?
Can you **turn on** the TV?

BOSS: **Would** you **answer** my phone for me, Marcia?
Could you **give** me a copy of the sales report?

---

2. Use *please* to make the request <u>more polite</u>. Note the word order.

• **Could** you *please* close the door?

OR

• **Could** you close the door, *please*?

---

3. We also use *Would you mind +* **gerund** to make polite requests. Note that a <u>negative answer</u> means that you <u>will do what the person requests</u>.

A: **Would you mind waiting** for a few minutes? Mr. Caras is still in a meeting.

B: *Not at all.*
(OK. I'll do it.)

---

4. People usually expect us to say *yes* to polite requests. When we **cannot say** *yes*, we usually <u>apologize and give a reason</u>.

▶ **BE CAREFUL!** Do not use *would* or *could* in response to polite requests.

A: **Could** you **take** this to Susan Lane's office for me?

B: **I'm sorry, I can't.** I'm expecting an important phone call.

A: I'm cold. **Would** you **shut** the window, please?

B: *Certainly.*
NOT ~~Yes, I would.~~

FOCUSED PRACTICE

1 DISCOVER THE GRAMMAR

Marcia has a new co-worker. Read their conversations. Underline all the polite requests.

1. MARCIA: Hi. You must be the new secretary. I'm Marcia Jones. Let me know if you need anything.

    LORNA: Thanks, Marcia. <u>Could you show</u> me the coat closet?

    MARCIA: Certainly. It's right over here.

2. LORNA: Marcia, would you explain these instructions for the fax machine? I don't understand them.

    MARCIA: Sure. Just put your letter in here and dial the number.

3. MARCIA: I'm leaving for lunch. Would you like to come?

    LORNA: Thanks, but I can't right now. I'm really busy.

    MARCIA: Do you want a sandwich from the coffee shop?

    LORNA: That would be great. Can you get me a tuna sandwich and a soda?

    MARCIA: Sure. Will you answer my phone until I get back?

    LORNA: Certainly.

4. MARCIA: Lorna, would you mind making a pot of coffee? Some clients are coming in a few minutes, and I make terrible coffee.

    LORNA: I'm sorry, but I can't do it now. I've got to finish this letter before 2:00.

    MARCIA: That's OK. Thanks anyway.

5. MARCIA: I'm going home now. Don't forget to turn off the printer before you leave.

    LORNA: I won't.

    MARCIA: By the way, I'm not coming to work tomorrow. Could you give this report to Joan Sanchez for me?

    LORNA: Sure.

2 ASKING FOR FAVORS   Grammar Notes 3 and 4

Mike's roommate, Jeff, is having problems today. Check the appropriate response to each request.

1. Mike, would you please drive me to class today? My car won't start.

    a. _____ Yes, I would.   **b.** __✔__ I'd be glad to.

2. Would you mind lending me five dollars? I'm getting paid tomorrow.

    a. _____ Not at all.   **b.** _____ Yes.

(continued on next page)

3. Mike, can you take these books back to the library for me? I'm running late this morning.

    a. _____ I'm late for class, too. Sorry.   **b.** _____ No, I can't.

4. Could you lock the door on your way out? My hands are full.

    a. _____ Yes, I could.   **b.** _____ Sure.

5. Can you turn the radio down? I need to study for my math quiz this morning.

    a. _____ Certainly.   **b.** _____ Not at all.

6. Will you pick up some milk on the way home this afternoon?

    a. _____ No, I won't.   **b.** _____ I'm sorry, I can't. I'll be at work until 8:00.

3 EDITING

Read Marcia Jones' response to an e-mail from her boss. (Her answers are in **bold** *print.) Find and correct six mistakes in making and responding to requests. The first mistake is already corrected.*

Subj: sales meeting—Reply
Date: 04-11-01 12:14:39 EST
From: MarciaJones@dataline.com
To: JohnSanchez@dataline.com
CC: AnnChen@dateline.com

>>> <JohnSanchez@dataline.com> 04/11/01 10:37am>>>

please call

The meetings are going well but they have been extended a day. Could you ~~call please~~ Doug Rogers to try to reschedule our sales meeting?

Not at all. I'll do it right away.

We'll need three extra copies of the monthly sales report. Would you ask Ann to take care of that?

Yes, I would. (Ann—could you do this?)

I hate to ask, but would you mind to work on Saturday? We'll need the extra time to go over the new information I've gotten.

Sorry, but I couldn't. My in-laws are coming for a visit. But Rob Lin says he can come in to the office to help out.

One last thing. I was going to pick up those new business cards, but I won't be back in time. Would you mind doing that for me?

Yes, I would. I'll stop at the printers during my lunch break.

4 WOULD YOU MIND?

Look at the pictures. What is each person thinking? Write the letter of the correct sentence from the box.

a. Buy some cereal.
b. Call back later.
c. Close the window.
d. ~~File these reports~~.
e. Shut the door.
f. Wait for a few minutes.

1. d

2.

3.

4.

5.

6.

What do the people say? Complete their polite requests. Use the words in parentheses and the information from the pictures.

1. _Can you please close the window?_ It's freezing in here.
   (Can)

2. _____ I've finished reading them.
   (Could)

3. _____ Mr. Rivera is still in a meeting.
   (Would you mind)

4. _____ on the way home? We don't have any left.
   (Will)

5. _____ Miss Sanchez is on another call right now.
   (Could)

6. _____ I can't think with all that noise in the hall.
   (Would)

COMMUNICATION PRACTICE

5 LISTENING

Marcia Jones has planned a busy weekend. Listen to the conversations. Then listen again and check the things that belong on her schedule.

__✔__ **a.** take Mark to the dentist

_____ **b.** take kids to the library

_____ **c.** babysit for Sally's daughter

_____ **d.** go to Sally's party

_____ **e.** go to the movies

_____ **f.** walk Mom's dog

_____ **g.** pick up the car at the garage

_____ **h.** go to the gym with Pat

6 I'D BE GLAD TO

Work in a group. Make out your own schedule for the weekend. Then ask group members to help you out. Use polite requests.

SATURDAY OCTOBER **18**	SUNDAY OCTOBER **19**
Morning _____	_____ Morning
Afternoon _____	_____ Afternoon
Evening _____	_____ Evening

EXAMPLE:

A: Can you drive me to the mall Saturday morning?

B: Sorry, I can't. I'm working Saturday morning.

> OR

Sure, I'd be glad to.

7 WRITING

Read the following situations. For each one, write a note making one or more requests.

1. Your roommate is going away for the weekend. Your sister from out of town will be visiting you. Write a note to your roommate.

   EXAMPLE:

   > Hi Viktor,
   >
   > My sister is visiting this weekend. Would you mind lending her your bike? I'd like to take her for a ride in the park.
   >
   > Thanks,
   >
   > Kunio

2. You work at a restaurant on Mondays, Wednesdays, and Fridays. You have to go to the dentist, but he or she can only see you on Wednesday. Write a note to a co-worker.

3. You're in school. You have to leave class early in order to help your parents. Write a note to a classmate.

4. You're going to have a party at your home. You've invited twenty people. Write a note to your neighbor.

14 ADVICE:
SHOULD, OUGHT TO,
HAD BETTER

GRAMMAR **IN CONTEXT**

BEFORE YOU READ Look at the photograph. What type of job is the woman training for? What skills does she need?

Read this page from an advertisement for Capital Training Institute.

Capital
Training Institute

Here are the answers to questions our students often ask:

Q: I can't go to college. Will I still find a job?

A: Many jobs don't require a college education. For example, administrative assistants and travel agents often move up to better positions. But be careful—you **shouldn't take** a job unless it offers you a good future. At Capital, you can get the skills you need for a job with a future.

Q: What are the best jobs these days?

A: For the next ten years, the best opportunities will be in service jobs. High school graduates **ought to think** about fields like health care and restaurant services.

Q: How **should** I **prepare** for a service job?

A: You will need a high school education for any good job. That means you**'d better not quit** high school if you want to get ahead. In fact, you **should plan** to get more education after you graduate. And, of course, computer skills are important for almost any job.

Q: I want to start my own business. **Should** I **get** a job first?

A: Yes. You **should** definitely **get** some experience before you start your own business. Appliance repairers and truck drivers often start their own companies after a few years on the job.

GRAMMAR **PRESENTATION**

ADVICE: *SHOULD, OUGHT TO, HAD BETTER*

	STATEMENTS		
SUBJECT	**SHOULD / OUGHT TO / HAD BETTER***	**BASE FORM OF VERB**	
I You He She We You They	**should (not)** **ought to** **had better (not)**	**look for**	a job.
		quit	school.

CONTRACTIONS	
should not	= **shouldn't**
had better	= **'d better**

*Should and *ought to* are modals. *Had better* is similar to a modal. These forms do not have -s in the third-person singular.

YES / NO QUESTIONS			
SHOULD	**SUBJECT**	**BASE FORM OF VERB**	
Should	I he she we they	**look for**	a job?
		quit	school?

SHORT ANSWERS		
AFFIRMATIVE		
Yes,	you he she you they	**should**.

SHORT ANSWERS		
NEGATIVE		
No,	you he she you they	**shouldn't**.

WH- QUESTIONS				
WH- WORD	**SHOULD**	**SUBJECT**	**BASE FORM OF VERB**	
How When Where	**should**	I he she we they	**prepare**	for a job?

NOTES

EXAMPLES

1. Use *should* and *ought to* to say that <u>something is advisable</u>.

- Fred and Tara **should answer** that want ad soon.
- They **ought to go** on some job interviews.

USAGE NOTE: We do not usually use the negative of *ought to* in American English. We use *shouldn't* instead.

- They **shouldn't wait**.
  NOT COMMON ~~They ought not to wait.~~

(continued on next page)

PRONUNCIATION NOTE
Ought to is often pronounced /ɔtə/ in informal speech.

2. Use *had better* for <u>urgent advice</u>—when you believe that something bad will happen if the person does not follow the advice.

- Kids, you**'d better leave** now, or you'll miss the school bus.

USAGE NOTE: The full form *had better* is very formal. We usually <u>use the contraction</u>.

- You**'d better apply** for more than one job.
  NOT <del>You had better apply . . .</del>

The negative of *had better* is **had better not**.

- You**'d better not be** late.
  NOT <del>You'd not better be late.</del>

▶ **BE CAREFUL!** *Had better* always refers to the <u>present</u> or the <u>future</u>, never to the past (even though it uses the word *had*).

- We**'d better take** the bus *now*.
- You**'d better call** them back *tomorrow*.

3. Use *should* for <u>questions</u>. We do not usually use *ought to* or *had better* for questions.

- *Should* I **go** to secretarial school?
- When *should* I **apply**?

4. It is usually considered impolite to <u>give advice to people</u> of equal or higher status (such as friends or bosses) unless they ask for it. However, it is polite to give advice to these people <u>when they ask for it</u>.

FRIEND: **Should** I **shake** hands with the interviewer?

YOU: Yes, you **should**.

BOSS: Where **should** I **take** our client to lunch?

YOU: I think you **should go** to the Tuscan Grill.

When we give <u>unasked-for advice</u>, we often soften it with *maybe*, *perhaps*, or *I think*.

- Myra, *maybe* you **ought to call** Capital Training Institute.

REFERENCE NOTE
Sometimes we use *must* or *have to* to give very <u>strong advice</u>. This kind of advice is similar to talking about necessity or obligation (*see Unit 33*).

FOCUSED PRACTICE

1 DISCOVER THE GRAMMAR

Two students are looking at the bulletin board at Capital Training Institute. Read their conversations and underline the words and phrases that give advice. Then complete each conversation with the number of the correct job notice.

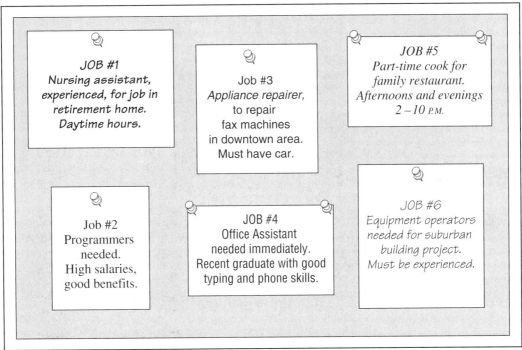

JOB #1
Nursing assistant, experienced, for job in retirement home. Daytime hours.

Job #3
Appliance repairer, to repair fax machines in downtown area. Must have car.

JOB #5
Part-time cook for family restaurant. Afternoons and evenings 2 – 10 P.M.

Job #2
Programmers needed. High salaries, good benefits.

JOB #4
Office Assistant needed immediately. Recent graduate with good typing and phone skills.

JOB #6
Equipment operators needed for suburban building project. Must be experienced.

1. **A:** Jake just finished a job for CTX builders. He's looking for work.

   B: He <u>should call</u> about number ___6___ . He's got a lot of experience now.

2. **A:** I want a part-time job this semester. I think I'll apply for number _____ .

   B: Maybe you shouldn't apply for that one. You have night classes, remember?

3. **A:** Pam quit her job at City Hospital because she couldn't work at night.

   B: She ought to apply for number _____ . Older people really like her.

4. **A:** The company offered Cindy number _____ .

   B: Well, she'd better not take it. She hates to drive in the city.

5. **A:** Kate and Denny are always complaining about their salaries.

   B: Programmers can make good money. They should call and find out about

   number _____ .

6. **A:** Tom's just finished his course in office administration.

   B: Really? We'd better tell him about number _____ . They need someone right away.

2 SHOULD'S AND SHOULD NOT'S Grammar Notes 1–2

Choose the correct words to complete this advice for job-seekers.

Want or need a new job? When's the best time to start looking? Right now! You

_____'d better not_____ delay, or you'll start to feel "stuck." These tips will help:
1. (ought to / 'd better not)

• A lot of people wait until after the holidays to look for a job. That means less

  competition for you. You _____ wait!
  2. (shouldn't / should)

• Too busy at work to schedule interviews? Early morning interviews have fewer

  interruptions. You _____ ask for interviews before nine o'clock.
  3. (should / 'd better not)

• If you are laid off, you _____ immediately take a lower-paying job just
  4. ('d better / shouldn't)

  to get work. If your salary is low, your employer won't appreciate your skills. If possible,

  you _____ wait and look for a salary that matches your skills.
  5. ('d better not / should)

• However, money isn't everything! You _____ take a position with a
  6. (ought to / 'd better not)

  company you dislike, or you won't do a good job there.

• The best way to ruin an interview is to talk about salary too soon. You

  _____ wait—learn about the job and talk about your skills first.
  7. ('d better / shouldn't)

3 FRIENDLY ADVICE Grammar Note 4

*Read the conversations. Write advice with **maybe**, **perhaps**, or **I think**. Use the*
words in parentheses. Choose between affirmative and negative statements.

1. **A:** I'm tired. I studied all weekend for my exam.

   B: ____Maybe you'd better not study all night.____ You need to rest.
          ('d better study all night)

2. **A:** I'm hungry. I haven't eaten since breakfast.

   B: _____ The snack bar is open now.
          (ought to have a sandwich)

3. **A:** I have a headache, but I just took two aspirins an hour ago.

   B: _____ Lie down instead.
          ('d better take another one)

4. **A:** My brother hasn't made any progress in English this semester.

   B: _____ Watching TV really helps my English.
          (should watch more TV)

5. **A:** I'm not earning enough money as a waitress.

   B: _____ Then you could find a better job.
          (should learn some new skills)

4 WHAT SHOULD I DO?

Kim Yee has just started working in the United States. His boss has invited him to dinner at his home, and Kim is asking his English teacher, Scott, some questions. Complete their conversation with **should, ought to,** *or* **had better** *and the words and phrases in parentheses. Choose between affirmative and negative forms.*

KIM: _____How should I dress?_____ In a suit?
            1. (How / dress?)

SCOTT: You don't have to wear a suit. I think _____, but you
                                                    2. (look / neat)

can wear casual clothes.

KIM: _____
            3. (What time / arrive?)

SCOTT: It's really important to be on time. They're expecting you at 7:00, so

_____. It's OK to be a little late, but don't make your
        4. (arrive after 7:15)

new boss wait too long for you!

KIM: _____
            5. (bring a gift?)

SCOTT: That's a good idea. But get something small. _____ It
                                                        6. (buy an expensive gift)

would embarrass him.

KIM: _____
            7. (What / buy?)

SCOTT: I think _____.
                    8. (get some flowers)

5 EDITING

Read this letter. Find and correct six mistakes in the use of modals that express advice. The first mistake is already corrected.

Dear Son,

We are so happy to hear about your new job. Congratulations! Just remember—you shouldn't ~~to~~ work too hard. The most important thing right now is your schoolwork. Maybe you only oughta work two days a week instead of three. Also, we think you'd better ask your boss for time off during exams. That way you'll have plenty of time to study. You would better give this a lot of careful thought, OK? Please take good care of yourself. You'd not better start skipping meals, and you definitely shouldn't worked at night. At your age, you will better get a good night's sleep. Do you need anything from home? Should we send any of your books? Let us know.

With love,

Mom and Dad

COMMUNICATION PRACTICE

6 LISTENING

A teacher at Capital Institute is giving his students advice about taking their final exam. Listen. Then listen again and check the sentences that agree with his advice.

___✔___ **1.** Sleep well the night before the test.

_____ **2.** Stay up late and study the night before the test.

_____ **3.** Sleep late and skip breakfast.

_____ **4.** Leave plenty of time to get to school.

_____ **5.** Start answering questions right away.

_____ **6.** Read the exam completely before you start.

_____ **7.** Do the difficult sections first.

_____ **8.** Be sure to finish the test.

7 NEW COUNTRY, NEW CUSTOMS

Work with a partner. Imagine that your partner has been offered a job in a country that you know very well. Give some advice about customs there. Then switch roles. Use the topics below and some of your own.

- Calling your boss by his or her first name

- Shaking hands when you first meet someone

- Calling a co-worker by a nickname

- Bringing a gift to your host or hostess

- Asking for a second helping of food when you are a guest

- Crossing the street before the light turns green

Add your own topics.

- _____

- _____

> **EXAMPLES:**
> You'd better not call your boss by her first name.
> You should shake hands when you first meet someone.

8 PROBLEM SOLVING

Work in small groups. Take turns telling each other about problems you are having. They can be real problems or invented problems, or you can choose from the examples below. Let the others in the group give advice.

EXAMPLES:

Problem: I'm having trouble making friends.

Advice: Maybe you should come to the students' lounge. I think you ought to spend more time with the rest of us . . .

Other problems: I don't think I'm earning enough money.
I don't have enough free time.

9 THIS PLACE NEEDS WORK!

Look at a classroom at Mo's Training Institute. Working in pairs, give advice for ways that Mo can improve his institute. Then compare your ideas with the ideas of another pair.

EXAMPLE:

A: He should empty the trash.

B: Yes, and he ought to . . .

10 WRITING

Look at Exercise 9. Imagine you are a student at Mo's Training Institute. Write a letter of complaint. Give advice on improvements Mo should make.

SUGGESTIONS:
LET'S, COULD, WHY DON'T . . . ?, WHY NOT . . . ?, HOW ABOUT . . . ?

GRAMMAR **IN CONTEXT**

BEFORE YOU READ What do you know about hosteling? Would you like to stay in one of the hostels pictured below?

 Read this youth hostel brochure.

Let's Travel!
HOSTELLING INTERNATIONAL

A LOT OF INTERNATIONAL STUDENTS WANT TO TRAVEL—but it's too expensive, or they don't want to travel alone.

Are you spending your vacation in the dorm? If so, **why don't** you **travel** and stay at youth hostels? Hosteling is cheap, and you'll meet friendly people from all over the world.

Altena Castle, Germany

There are more than 6,000 hostels in over 70 different countries. They vary from simple buildings to magnificent old castles such as the Altena castle in Germany.

Do you like cities? **Why not stay** at the Ma Wai Hall overlooking the harbor in exciting Hong Kong? Or **maybe** you **could spend** the night at the historic Clay Hotel in Miami Beach. (Gangsters used to meet there.)

Tired of being on land? **How about a room** on the *af Chapman* in Stockholm, Sweden? Built in 1888, this sailing ship has been rocking tired hostelers to sleep for more than fifty years.

Wherever you go, you'll meet talkative travelers, share stories with them, and gain a greater understanding of the world and its people. So what are you waiting for?

LET'S GO!

af Chapman, Sweden

GRAMMAR **PRESENTATION**
SUGGESTIONS: *LET'S, COULD, WHY DON'T . . . ?,*
WHY NOT . . . ?, HOW ABOUT . . . ?

LET'S

LET'S (NOT)	BASE FORM OF VERB	
Let's (not)	take	the ferry.
	stay	in a castle.

COULD

(MAYBE)	SUBJECT	COULD*	BASE FORM OF VERB	
(Maybe)	I you he she we they	could	take	the ferry.
			stay	in a castle.

Could is a modal. Modals have only one form. They do not have -*s* in the third-person singular.

WHY DON'T . . . ?

WHY	DON'T / DOESN'T	SUBJECT	BASE FORM OF VERB	
Why	don't	I we you they	take	the ferry?
	doesn't	he she	stay	in the castle?

WHY NOT . . . ?

WHY NOT	BASE FORM OF VERB	
Why not	take	the ferry?
	stay	in a castle?

HOW ABOUT . . . ?

HOW ABOUT	GERUND / NOUN	
How about	staying	in the castle?
	the castle?	

NOTES	**EXAMPLES**
1. Use *Let's, (Maybe) . . . could, Why don't / doesn't, Why not,* and *How about* to make <u>suggestions</u>.	**A:** *Let's* **take** a trip this summer. **B:** *Maybe* we *could* **go** to Costa Rica. **A:** *Why don't* we **ask** Luke to go with us? **B:** Good idea. *Why doesn't* Tom **call** him tonight? **A:** *Why not* **call** him right now? **B:** *How about* **staying** at youth hostels? **A:** Yes. *How about* **the hostel** in the rain forest?
USAGE NOTE: We usually use these expressions when we are speaking in <u>informal situations</u> or in an informal note or letter. We don't usually use them in formal situations.	**INFORMAL** • *Why don't* you visit Paris? **FORMAL** • May I suggest that you visit Paris?
▶ **BE CAREFUL!** When someone uses *Why not* and *Why don't / doesn't* to <u>make a suggestion</u>, these expressions are not information questions. The speaker does <u>not expect to receive information</u> from the listener.	**SUGGESTION** **A:** *Why don't* you **visit** Jill in New York? **B:** That's a good idea. **INFORMATION QUESTION** **A:** *Why don't* you **eat** meat? **B:** Because I'm a vegetarian.

2. *Let's* always <u>includes the speaker</u>. It means *Here's a suggestion for you and me.*	• *Let's* **go** to Miami. We need a vacation. *(I suggest that we go to Miami.)* • *Let's* **not** **stay** at a hostel. *(I suggest that we don't stay at a hostel.)*

3. Note the **different forms** to use with these expressions.

BASE FORM OF THE VERB
- *Let's* **take** the ferry.
- *Maybe* we *could* **take** the ferry.
- *Why don't* we **take** the ferry to Hong Kong island?
- *Why doesn't* she **take** the ferry to Hong Kong island?
- *Why not* **take** the ferry?

GERUND OR A NOUN
- *How about* **taking** the ferry?
- *How about* **the ferry**?

4. Notice the **punctuation** at the end of each kind of suggestion.

STATEMENTS
- *Let's* go to a concert.
- *Maybe* we *could* go to a concert.

QUESTIONS
- *Why don't* we go to a concert**?**
- *Why not* go to a concert**?**
- *How about* going to a concert**?**
- *How about* a concert**?**

REFERENCE NOTE
Making suggestions is sometimes similar to giving advice. *(See Unit 14.)*

FOCUSED PRACTICE

1 DISCOVER THE GRAMMAR

Emily and Megan are visiting Hong Kong. Read their conversation.
Underline all the suggestions.

EMILY: <u>Why don't we go to the races?</u> I hear they're really exciting.

MEGAN: I'd like to, but I need to go shopping.

EMILY: Then let's go to the Temple Street Market tonight. We might even see some Chinese opera in the street while we're there.

MEGAN: That sounds like fun. If we do that, why not go to the races this afternoon?

EMILY: OK, but let's get something to eat first in one of those floating restaurants.

MEGAN: I don't think we'll have time. Maybe we could do that tomorrow. Right now, how about getting *dim sum* at the Kau Kee Restaurant next door? Then we could take the Star Ferry to Hong Kong Island and the racecourse.

EMILY: Sounds good. Here's an idea for tomorrow. Why not take one of those small boats—*kaido*—to Lantau Island? When we come back, we could have dinner at the Jumbo Palace.

MEGAN: Let's do that. It's a little expensive, but it floats.

Now look at this page from a Hong Kong guidebook and check the places Emily and Megan will visit and the transportation they will take.

Hong Kong Highlights

- ◆ **Hong Kong Space Museum.** One of the world's most advanced. See the Sky Show and a movie on the Omnimax movie screen.
- ✔◆ **Temple Street Night Market.** Find great bargains, visit a fortuneteller, and, with luck, hear Chinese opera performed in the street.

- ◆ **Harbour City.** Shop for clothing, electronics, and antiques in this huge, modern mall. Beautiful harbor views from the open rooftop.
- ◆ **Happy Valley Racecourse.** Watch Hong Kong's favorite sport. Feel the excitement as millions of Hong Kong dollars ride on every race.

Transportation

- ◆ **Railway lines** make local stops in both Kowloon and on Hong Kong Island. Use the Kwung Tong Line in Kowloon and the Island Line on Hong Kong Island.
- ◆ **The Star Ferry** is the queen of Hong Kong water transportation, and it's a bargain, too. There are several routes connecting Kowloon and Hong Kong Island.
- ◆ **Kaido** are small wooden ferries that carry 20–40 passengers.

Places to Eat

- ◆ **Jumbo Palace** ($$$) A traditional-style floating restaurant specializing in seafood.
- ◆ **Broadway Seafood Restaurant** ($) A friendly restaurant. Try the fresh scallops in black bean sauce.
- ◆ **Kau Kee Restaurant** ($) A favorite place for *dim sum*—a great way to try a variety of dishes.

2 MAKING PLANS

Complete the conversations with the appropriate expression in parentheses.

1. A: I feel like having seafood for dinner, but we went to Tai Pak for seafood last night.

   B: _____Why not_____ go again? The food's great, and so is the view.
           (Why not / Let's not)

2. A: I'm really tired. _____ resting before we go out?
                           (Let's / How about)

   B: That's a good idea. I'm tired, too.

3. A: I want to explore downtown Hong Kong.

   B: _____ take a minibus? We'll see a lot more that way.
       (Let's not / Why don't we)

4. A: A group of foreign students just checked into the hostel.

   B: _____ ask them to join us for dinner.
       (How about / Maybe we could)

5. A: I don't want to go home tomorrow. I'm having a really good time here.

   B: So am I. _____ leave tomorrow.
           (Let's / Let's not)

3 LET'S . . .

Complete the suggestions with phrases from the box. Add pronouns and change the verbs as necessary. Punctuate correctly.

take a trip together	try that new seafood place	~~buy tickets~~
go to the beach	buy another one	

1. A: There's an Oasis concert at the Hong Kong Convention Centre next weekend.

   B: We're near there now. Why don't _____ we buy tickets? _____

2. A: It's going to be hot tomorrow.

   B: I know. How about _____

3. A: Sweaters are on sale. Maybe we could buy one for Brian's birthday.

   B: We got him a sweater last year. Let's not _____

4. A: I don't know what to do on spring vacation. I'm sick of staying in the dorm.

   B: Me too. Maybe _____

5. A: I'm hungry.

   B: Let's _____

COMMUNICATION PRACTICE

4 LISTENING

Emily and Megan have just arrived on Lantau Island in Hong Kong. Look at the map. Then, listen to the conversation. Listen again. On the map, check the things they decide to do and places they decide to see.

The S. G. Davis Hostel

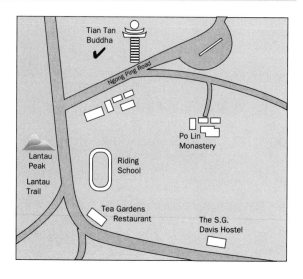

5 HOW ABOUT . . . ?

Work with a partner. Imagine you are both visiting Hong Kong. Look at the guidebook on page 154 and talk about what you like to do or want to do. Make suggestions about activities.

> **EXAMPLE:**
> **A:** I want to buy some souvenirs.
> **B:** Let's go to the Temple Street Night Market.

6 THINGS TO DO

Work with a group to plan a trip to an interesting place in your area. Discuss the following:

• where to go	• how to get there	• who will call or write
• when to go	• what to do there	for more information

> **EXAMPLES:**
> How about visiting San Diego?   Why not take the bus?
> Maybe we could go next weekend.   Why don't the two of you call
> How about going to the zoo?   for information?

7 WRITING

Write a letter to someone who is going to visit you. Make suggestions about the things you can do together.

REVIEW OR SELFTEST

I. *Circle the letter of the appropriate response to each question.*

1. Could you speak English when you were a child?
   a. I'd be glad to.
   b. Yes, I could.

2. Can you swim?
   a. Yes, I can. I'd be glad to.
   b. Yes, I can. I really enjoy it.

3. Would you turn off the lights before you leave?
   a. Of course.
   b. Yes, I would.

4. May I ask a question?
   a. Yes, you may. What is it?
   b. You may. I'm not sure.

5. Would you mind lending me some money? I left my wallet at home.
   a. Yes, I would. Here's $10.
   b. Not at all. Here's $10.

6. Why don't we go to the beach today?
   a. Good idea.
   b. Because the car broke down.

7. Could you explain this word to me?
   a. Sorry, but I don't understand it, either.
   b. No, I couldn't. I never heard it before!

8. Maybe I'll wear a suit. What do you think?
   a. Maybe you shouldn't.
   b. Maybe you won't.

II. *Read each sentence. Write its function. Use the words in the box.*

ability	advice	permission	request	suggestion

1. Could I call you tonight? ____permission____

2. Could you please turn the light out before you leave? _____

3. Why not take the train? _____

(continued on next page)

4. Of course you can use my pen. _____

5. When Eva was little, she couldn't reach the elevator button. _____

6. Do you mind if my sister comes with us? _____

7. Let's take a taxi. _____

8. You'd better work harder or you won't pass your test. _____

9. Would you mind calling back in about half an hour? _____

10. Will you please explain that to me again? _____

11. I can't lift that box by myself. _____

12. Maybe we could go to a later movie. _____

III. *Circle the correct words to complete the conversations.*

1. **A:** This apartment is depressing me.

   B: <u>May we</u> / (<u>Why not</u>) redecorate? We have some free time.
         1.

   A: OK. Where <u>should we / were we able to</u> start?
               2.

   B: Maybe we <u>could / couldn't</u> start with the hall. It's easy to put up wallpaper.
             3.

   A: How much wallpaper do we need?

   B: We <u>can't / 'd better</u> measure the walls and find out.
           4.

   A: This wallpaper is pretty. <u>Let's / How about</u> start putting it up.
               5.

   B: We <u>may / should</u> clean the walls first.
          6.

   A: OK. The walls are clean. <u>How about / Can</u> putting up the wallpaper now?
               7.

2. **A:** Dancing Wheels is performing at City Center next weekend. <u>Let's / Would you mind</u>
                                                   1.

     get tickets.

   B: Good idea. <u>Could / Should</u> you pick them up? I'm really busy this week.
                2.

   A: No problem. I'll <u>can / be able to</u> get them after class today.
                 3.

     <u>Do you mind if / How about</u> I get a ticket for Carlos, too?
            4.

   B: <u>Yes, I do. / Not at all.</u> I haven't seen him in ages. Maybe we <u>could / will</u> all go out
         5.   6.

     to dinner before the theater. I hear that new Indian restaurant is very good.

   A: OK, but we <u>could / 'd better</u> make a reservation. It's very popular.
                7.

3. A: I'm taking the TOEFL exam this year. Any suggestions?

   B: <u>How about / Why don't</u> you ask Anatol? He took it last year.
               1.

   A: Good idea. <u>Could / Should</u> you give me his phone number?
                2.

   B: I don't have it, but you <u>'d better / could</u> ask Karin. She'll have it.
                        3.

   A: <u>Do you mind if / Would you mind</u> asking her for me? You know her better than I do.
               4.

   B: Sure.

IV. *Each sentence has four underlined words or phrases. The four underlined parts of the sentences are marked A, B, C, or D. Circle the letter of the <u>one</u> underlined word or phrase that is NOT CORRECT.*

1. <u>When</u> I was young, I <u>could</u> hit a baseball very far, but I <u>wasn't</u> able   **A B C Ⓓ**
   A   B   C
<u>run</u> fast.
 D

2. Why <u>don't</u> we <u>have</u> dinner and then <u>go</u> see *Possible Dreams.*   **A B C D**
     A   B   C   D

3. You <u>drove</u> for seven hours today, so <u>maybe</u> you'd <u>not better</u>   **A B C D**
      A   B   C
<u>drive</u> tonight.
 D

4. <u>Will</u> you mind <u>bringing</u> your camera to the graduation party   **A B C D**
   A   B
<u>tomorrow</u> <u>?</u>
   C   D

5. Dad, <u>may</u> I <u>borrow</u> the car tomorrow or <u>does</u> Mom <u>has</u> to use it?   **A B C D**
      A   B   C   D

6. I <u>can't</u> <u>help</u> you with this math problem, so <u>maybe</u> you should <u>to talk</u>   **A B C D**
   A   B   C   D
to your teacher tomorrow.

7. <u>Should</u> I <u>bring</u> flowers for my host tonight, or <u>should</u> I <u>giving</u> her   **A B C D**
   A   B   C   D
something more expensive?

8. <u>May be</u> you <u>ought</u> <u>to</u> just <u>bring</u> flowers.   **A B C D**
   A   B   C   D

9. Silva <u>wasn't</u> a strong child, but she <u>could</u> win first prize in gymnastics   **A B C D**
       A   B
<u>when</u> she <u>was</u> ten.
  C   D

10. <u>I maybe</u> <u>will</u> be able <u>to</u> <u>finish</u> my homework early tonight.   **A B C D**
    A   B   C D

11. <u>It's</u> really late, so <u>let's</u> <u>us</u> <u>go</u> out to dinner tonight, OK?   **A B C D**
    A   B   C D

V. *Find and correct the mistake in each conversation.*

1. **A:** Can Elena ~~dances~~? *dance*

   B: Yes, she's great. She's able to do all kinds of difficult steps.

2. **A:** When you were a child, were you able to skate?

   B: Yes. In fact, I once could win a competition in my school.

3. **A:** Could please you help me?

   B: Sure. What seems to be the problem?

4. **A:** Would you mind giving me a ride home?

   B: Yes, I would. When would you like to leave?

5. **A:** We really ought see the movie that's playing at the Quad.

   B: OK. Let's go Friday night.

6. **A:** We would better hurry, or we'll be late.

   B: Don't worry. We can still get there on time.

7. **A:** Could I borrow the car tonight?

   B: Sorry, but you couldn't. I need it myself.

8. **A:** Do you mind if my friend coming to the party with me?

   B: Not at all. There's always room for one more!

▶ *To check your answers, go to the Answer Key on page 163.*

FROM GRAMMAR TO WRITING USING APPROPRIATE MODALS

When you write a note, you do more than give information. You perform social functions such as asking for permission and making requests. Modals help you perform these functions politely.

EXAMPLE:
I want you to call me in the morning. ⟶
Could you **please** call me in the morning?

1 *Read this note from Ed to his co-worker, Chen. Work with a partner and decide which sentences should have modals. Underline the sentences.*

From The Desk of Ed Hansen . . .

Chen,

Here is our project summary. <u>Read it.</u> I think it's too long. What do you think? Tell me whether to shorten it. We will meet tomorrow to discuss it. My advice is that we finish the draft by Friday. By the way, Nadia is in town. I want to invite her to our meeting.

Ed

---

2 *Complete a second draft of the note. Use modals to express the functions in parentheses.*

From The Desk of Ed Hansen . . .

Chen,

Here is our project summary. <u>Would you mind</u> reading it? I think
               (make a request)
it's too long. What do you think? _____ I shorten it?
                         (ask advice)
_____ meet tomorrow to discuss it. We _____
(make a suggestion)   (give advice)
finish the final draft by Friday. By the way, Nadia is in town.

_____ I invite her to our meeting?
(ask permission)

Ed

---

3 *Complete Chen's note to Ed. Use modals to express the following ideas:*

- Shorten the summary. (advice)
- I want to meet tomorrow morning instead. (suggestion)
- Reserve the conference room for the meeting. (request)
- Of course Nadia will come to the meeting. (permission)
- We're going to have lunch together after the meeting. (suggestion)

From the Desk of Chen Wu . . .

Ed—

Sorry, I was very busy this morning, so I wasn't able to finish reading the summary until now.

I think you should shorten it.

_____

_____

_____

_____

See you tomorrow morning.

Chen

---

4 *Before you write . . .*

- Work with a partner. Choose one of the situations below. Role-play the situation. Use modals to express the ideas.

a. You work in a sales office. Recently a customer complained to your boss because he had to wait for service. You want to meet with your boss to explain what happened. You'd like to bring a co-worker who saw the incident. You think the company needs another receptionist for busy times.

b. You would like your English teacher to write a letter of recommendation for you. You want her to mention that you have good computer skills and are an A student in her class. You're not sure how many hours to work a week, so you ask her. You want to miss class so that you can go to your job interview.

- Work with another pair of partners. Watch their role play. Make a list of functions they expressed and the modals they used to express those functions. Discuss your list with them—did they express what they wanted to?

- Perform your role play and discuss it with the other pair.

5 *Write a note as one of the characters in the role play. Use social modals and information from the feedback you received from your role play.*

REVIEW OR SELFTEST
ANSWER KEY

I. (Units 11–15)

2. b	**6.** a
3. a	**7.** a
4. a	**8.** a
5. b	

II. (Units 11–15)

2. request	**8.** advice
3. suggestion	**9.** request
4. permission	**10.** request
5. ability	**11.** ability
6. permission	**12.** suggestion
7. suggestion	

III. (Units 11–15)

CONVERSATION 1

2. should we	**5.** Let's
3. could	**6.** should
4. 'd better*	**7.** How about

CONVERSATION 2

1. Let's	**5.** Not at all.
2. Could	**6.** could
3. be able to	**7.** 'd better
4. Do you mind if	

CONVERSATION 3

1. Why don't
2. Could
3. could
4. Would you mind

IV. (Units 11–15)

2. D	**7.** D
3. C	**8.** A
4. A	**9.** B
5. D	**10.** A
6. D	**11.** C

*Where a contracted form is given,
the long form is also correct.

V. (Units 11–15)

2. A: When you were a child, were
you able to skate?

B: Yes. In fact, I once ~~could~~ ^{was able to} win a
competition in my school.

3. A: Could ^{you please} ~~please you~~ help me?
  OR
  Could you help me, please?

B: Sure. What seems to be the
problem?

4. A: Would you mind giving me a
ride home?

B: ~~Yes, I would.~~ ^{Not at all. OR No, I wouldn't.} When would you
like to leave?

5. A: We really ought ^{to} see the movie
that's playing at the Quad.

B: OK. Let's go Friday night.

6. A: We ~~would~~ ^{'d} better hurry, or we'll
be late.

B: Don't worry. We can still get
there on time.

7. A: Could I borrow the car tonight?

B: Sorry, but you ~~couldn't~~ ^{can't}. I need
it myself.

8. A: Do you mind if my friend
~~coming~~ ^{comes} to the party with me?

B: Not at all. There's always room
for one more!

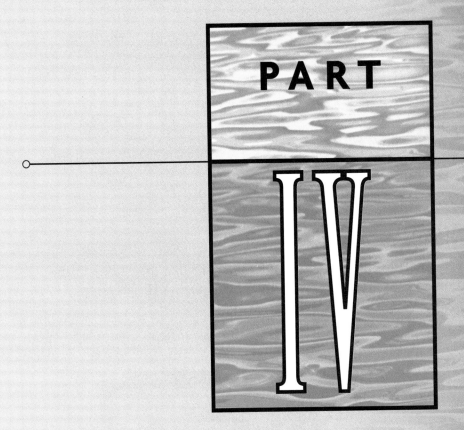

PART

IV

PRESENT PERFECT

PRESENT PERFECT: SINCE AND FOR

GRAMMAR IN CONTEXT

BEFORE YOU READ   Where can you find an article like this? Look at the information next to the photo. How long has Martina Hingis been a professional?

Read this article about tennis player Martina Hingis.

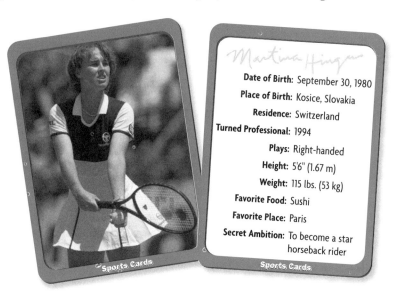

Date of Birth: September 30, 1980
Place of Birth: Kosice, Slovakia
Residence: Switzerland
Turned Professional: 1994
Plays: Right-handed
Height: 5'6" (1.67 m)
Weight: 115 lbs. (53 kg)
Favorite Food: Sushi
Favorite Place: Paris
Secret Ambition: To become a star horseback rider

Martina Hingis first picked up a tennis racket at the age of two. **Since then,** she **has become** one of the greatest tennis players in the world. Martina was born in Slovakia, but she and her mother **have lived** in Switzerland **for many years.** Martina became the outdoor Swiss champion at age nine. Then, in 1993, she became the youngest person ever to win the French Open Junior title. In 1996, she was the youngest player ever to win a Wimbledon event (Women's Doubles). A year later, she won almost all the major international tournaments—Wimbledon, the U.S. Open, and both singles and doubles matches at the Australian Open.

Many people criticize the lifestyle of very young tennis stars like Martina. Martina, for example, **hasn't attended** school **since 1994,** the year she turned professional. **Since then,** she **has played** tennis all over the world and **has earned** millions of dollars. As a result, she speaks several languages (English is her language on the court), and she is famous for her self-confidence. But what about a *normal* childhood? Like any young person, Martina enjoys shopping, going to parties, and listening to music. Tennis, however, **has been** the most important part of her life **since she was a little girl.** As she once told a reporter, "the life I'm living right now playing tennis is normal."

GRAMMAR **PRESENTATION**
PRESENT PERFECT: *SINCE* AND *FOR*

STATEMENTS

SUBJECT	HAVE / HAS (NOT)	PAST PARTICIPLE OF VERB		SINCE / FOR
I You* We They	**have (not)**	**been†** **lived**	here	**since** May. **for** a long time.
He She It	**has (not)**			

YES / NO QUESTIONS

HAVE / HAS	SUBJECT	PAST PARTICIPLE OF VERB		SINCE / FOR
Have	I you* we they	**been†** **lived**	here	**since** May? **for** a long time?
Has	he she it			

SHORT ANSWERS

AFFIRMATIVE		
Yes,	you I / we you they	**have.**
	he she it	**has.**

SHORT ANSWERS

NEGATIVE		
No,	you I / we you they	**haven't.**
	he she it	**hasn't.**

WH- QUESTIONS

WH- WORD	HAVE / HAS	SUBJECT	PAST PARTICIPLE	
How long	**have**	I you* we they	**been†** **lived**	here?
	has	he she it		

SHORT ANSWERS

Since January.
For a few months.

*You is both singular and plural.
†Been is an irregular past participle. See Grammar Notes on page 169 and Appendix 1 on page A-1 for a list of irregular verbs.

CONTRACTIONS

AFFIRMATIVE			
I have	= **I've**	he has	= **he's**
you have	= **you've**	she has	= **she's**
we have	= **we've**	it has	= **it's**
they have	= **they've**		

CONTRACTIONS

NEGATIVE	
have not	= **haven't**
has not	= **hasn't**

NOTES	EXAMPLES

1. Use the **present perfect** with *since or for* to talk about something that began in the past <u>and continues into the present</u> (and may continue into the future).

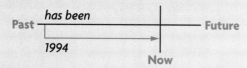

- Martina **has been** a professional tennis player *since* 1994.
- She **has been** a professional tennis player *for* several years.
  (She began her professional career several years ago, and she is still a professional player.)

---

2. Use the present perfect with *since + point in time (since 5:00, since Monday, since 1994, since yesterday)* to show <u>when something started</u>.

- She **has earned** millions of dollars *since 1994*.

---

3. *Since* can also introduce a **time clause**.

When the action in the time clause ended in the past, use the <u>simple past tense</u>.

When the action in the time clause began in the past but continues to the present, use the <u>present perfect</u>.

- Martina **has loved** sports *since she was a child*.
- She **has won** many tournaments *since she moved* from Slovakia.
  (She doesn't live there anymore.)
- She **has become** very successful *since she has been* in Switzerland.
  (She still lives in Switzerland.)

---

4. Use the present perfect with *for + length of time (for ten minutes, for two weeks, for years, for a long time)* to show <u>how long a present condition has lasted</u>.

- Martina's mother **has been** her coach *for many years*.

5. The present perfect is formed with *have* or *has* + past participle.

The **regular form of the past participle** is the base form of the verb + *-d* or *-ed.* This form is the same as the regular simple past form of the verb.

There are many **irregular past participles**. Some common ones are listed below.

(See Appendix 1, page A-1, for a more complete list.)

- She *has* **lived** there for years.

- They *have* **played** together many times since 1998.

- She *has* **bought** two new rackets since March.
- They *haven't* **won** a tournament for several years.

BASE FORM OF THE VERB	PAST PARTICIPLE	BASE FORM OF THE VERB	PAST PARTICIPLE
be	**been**	come	**came**
see	**seen**	do	**done**
bring	**brought**	go	**gone**
buy	**bought**	win	**won**
meet	**met**	drive	**driven**
sleep	**slept**	eat	**eaten**
hang	**hung**	get	**gotten**
sing	**sung**	give	**given**
sell	**sold**	take	**taken**
tell	**told**	write	**written**
put	**put**	find	**found**
read	**read**	have	**had**
run	**ran**	make	**made**

FOCUSED PRACTICE

1 DISCOVER THE GRAMMAR

Read the information about Gigi and Emilio. Then circle the letter of the sentence (**a** *or* **b**) *that best describes the situation.*

1. Gigi has been a tennis player since 1995.
    a. She still is a tennis player.
    b. She is not a tennis player anymore.

2. Gigi has had long hair since she was a little girl.
    a. She has short hair now.
    b. She has long hair now.

3. Gigi has lived in the same apartment for ten years.
    a. She lived in a different apartment eleven years ago.
    b. She moved a few years ago.

4. Gigi and Emilio have been married for twenty-five years.
    a. They got married twenty-five years ago.
    b. They are not married now.

5. Gigi and Emilio haven't been on a vacation since 1996.
    a. They were on a vacation in 1996.
    b. They are on a vacation now.

6. Gigi hasn't won a tennis championship for two years.
    a. She won a championship two years ago.
    b. She didn't win a championship two years ago.

2 WINNERS
Grammar Charts

Look at these tennis sports statistics. Use short answers to answer the questions.

YEAR	MEN	WOMEN
\multicolumn{3}{c}{**AUSTRALIAN OPEN DOUBLES CHAMPIONS**}		
1998	Jonas Bjorkman and Jacco Eltingh	Martina Hingis and Mirjana Lucic
1997	Todd Woodbridge and Mark Woodforde	Martina Hingis and Natasha Zvereva
1996	Stefan Edberg and Petr Korda	Chanda Rubin and Arantxa Sanchez Vicario
1995	Jared Palmer and Richey Reneberg	Jana Novotna and Arantxa Sanchez Vicario
1994	Jacco Eltingh and Paul Haarhuis	Gigi Fernandez and Natasha Zvereva
1993	Danie Visser and Laurie Warder	Gigi Fernandez and Natasha Zvereva
1992	Todd Woodbridge and Mark Woodforde	Arantxa Sanchez Vicario and Helevna Sukova

1. Martina Hingis won the Australian Open Doubles Championship in 1997.
    Has she won again since then?

    <u>Yes, she has.</u>

2. Danie Visser won the Australian Open Doubles Championship in 1993. Has he won again since then?

_____

3. Arantxa Sanchez Vicario won in 1992. Has she won again since then?

_____

4. Jared Palmer and Richey Reneberg won the Australian Open Doubles Championship in 1995. Have they won again since then?

_____

5. Helevna Sukova won in 1992. Has she won again since then?

_____

6. Gigi Fernandez and Natasha Zvereva won in 1993. Have they won as partners since then?

_____

7. Todd Woodbridge won in 1992. Has he won again since then?

_____

3 CHILD GENIUS

Grammar Notes 1–4

Read this magazine excerpt and complete it with **since** *or* **for**.

Thirteen-year-old Ronnie Segal has loved math ____*since*____ he was a little boy.
1.

"I have been interested in numbers _____ nine years, five months, three weeks, and
2.

two days," says Ronnie. _____ the past year, Ronnie has attended graduate-level
3.

classes at the university. _____ January he has taken five exams and has gotten
4.

grades of 100 on all of them. _____
5.

Ronnie began classes, he has met an average

of 1.324 people a month. And his future?

Thirteen-year-old Ronnie has known

_____ years that he is
6.

going to become a famous

sports announcer, get married,

and have exactly 2.2 children.

MARTINA HAS SERVED 52.3% OF THE TIME. SHE HAS WON 81% OF HER 1st SERVES AND 7.8% OF HER 2nd SERVES.

4 **A RESUME**

Ingrid Schwab is applying for a job as a college sports instructor. Look at her resume and the interviewer's notes. Complete the interview. Use the words in parentheses to write questions. Then answer the questions. The year is 2004.

Ingrid Schwab
2136 East Travis Street
San Antonio, Texas 78284

Education:

INTERVIEWED
09/11/04

1996 Certificate (American College of Sports Medicine)
1995 MA Physical Education (University of Texas)

moved to San Antonio in 1989

Employment:

1995—present   part-time physical education teacher
(high school)

1993—present   sports trainer (private)

teaches tennis, swimming

Skills:

speak Spanish, German, and Korean

martial arts   *—got black belt in Tae Kwon Do 2 mos. ago*

Awards:

1996 Teacher of the Year Award

1993 Silver Medal in Texas Tennis Competition

Memberships:

1996–present   member of National Education Association (NEA)

---

1. (How long / live in San Antonio?)

INTERVIEWER: How long have you lived in San Antonio?

INGRID: I've lived in San Antonio for 15 years.

OR

I've lived in San Antonio since 1989.

2. (How long / have your MA degree?)

INTERVIEWER: _____

INGRID: _____

3. (have any more training since you got your MA?)

    INTERVIEWER: _____

    INGRID: _____

4. (How long / be a physical education teacher?)

    INTERVIEWER: _____

    INGRID: _____

5. (How long / work as a sports trainer?)

    INTERVIEWER: _____

    INGRID: _____

6. (How long / have a black belt in Tae Kwon Do?)

    INTERVIEWER: _____

    INGRID: _____

7. (win any awards since then?)

    INTERVIEWER: I see you won a tennis award. _____

    INGRID: _____. I won the Teacher of the Year Award in 1996.

8. (How long / be a member of the NEA?)

    INTERVIEWER: _____

    INGRID: _____

5 EDITING

Read this student's journal entry. Find and correct nine mistakes in the use of the present perfect. The first mistake is already corrected.

>   *learned*
> I've ~~learn~~ a lot since Ms. Schwab became my teacher. I've been in her physical education
> class since two months. I've only miss two classes since the beginning of the semester.
> I've became a much better player since Ms. Schwab started teaching us. We don't play
> much since November because the weather have been too cold. Instead, we switched to
> volleyball. My team has winned two games since we started to compete. Next month
> we start swimming. I've been afraid of the water since many years, but now I think I can
> learn to swim. I got so confident since I've been in this class.

COMMUNICATION PRACTICE

6 LISTENING

Antonio Serrano is looking for a job as a radio sports announcer. Listen to this interview. Then, listen again and complete the interviewer's notes. Use **since** *and* **for**.

WSPR Radio

Antonio Serrano   interviewed 9/11

He's been a sports announcer ___for 20 years___.
　　　　　　　　　　　　　　　　　　　a.

He's had 2 jobs _____.
　　　　　　　　　　　b.

He's lived in Los Angeles _____.
　　　　　　　　　　　　　　　　c.

He hasn't worked _____.
　　　　　　　　　　d.

He's been a student at UCLA _____.
　　　　　　　　　　　　　　　　　e.

---

7 THE BEST PERSON FOR THE JOB

A business college needs a new math teacher. Look at these two resumes. In small groups, decide who to hire and why. Use **since** *and* **for**.

EXAMPLE:

A: Wu Hao has had the same job since he got his PhD.

B: Erika Jones has a lot of experience. She's been a teacher since 1976.

Wu Hao

Education:
1990 PhD in Mathematics (UCLA)

Teaching Experience:
1990–present Bryant College

Courses Taught:
Algebra
Trigonometry
Calculus
Business Mathematics

Publications:
"Introducing Computers into the College Math Class" (*The Journal of Mathematics*, 1992)

Awards:
Teacher of the Year, 1992
Distinguished Professor, 1999

Erika Jones

Education:
1976 PhD in Mathematics (UCLA)

Teaching Experience:
1996–present NYC Technical College
1991–1995   UCLA
1982–1990   University of Wisconsin, Madison
1979–1981   Brown University
1976–1978   UCLA

Courses Taught:
Mathematical Analysis 1
Mathematical Analysis 2

Publications:
"Imaginary Numbers" (*MJS*, 1981)
"Number Theory" (*Mathematics*, 1981)
"How Real Are Real Numbers?" (*Math Education*, 1984)

8 ROLE PLAY: A JOB INTERVIEW

Write a resume. Use Ingrid's resume on page 172 as a model. You can use real or imaginary information. Then, role-play a job interview with a partner. Take turns being the interviewer and the candidate. Use the script below to help you complete the interview.

EXAMPLE:

A: How long have you been a lab technician?

B: I've been a lab technician for five years.

INTERVIEWER: How long have you been a(n) _____ ?

CANDIDATE: I've _____

INTERVIEWER: And how many jobs have you had since _____ ?

CANDIDATE: I've _____

INTERVIEWER: I see from your resume that you live in _____
How long have you lived there?

CANDIDATE: _____

INTERVIEWER: Your English is quite good. How long have you studied it?

CANDIDATE: _____

INTERVIEWER: How long _____ ?

CANDIDATE: _____

INTERVIEWER: Well, thank you very much. We'll be in touch with you.

9 WRITING

*Write a paragraph about someone's accomplishments. It can be someone famous or someone you know. Use the present perfect with **since** or **for**.*

EXAMPLE:

Ingrid has been a high school physical education teacher and a private sports trainer for many years. She has received two awards since 1993, one for teaching and the other for tennis. She has been a member of the National Education Association since 1996. Ingrid speaks four languages. She has been a student of martial arts for a long time, and she has had her black belt in Tae Kwon Do since the summer.

PRESENT PERFECT: ALREADY AND YET

GRAMMAR IN CONTEXT

BEFORE YOU READ Look at the chart and the cartoon. What do you think this interview is about? What is happening in the cartoon?

Read this transcript of a television interview.

TOM: Good morning! I'm Tom Mendez, and this is "A.M. America." Dr. Helmut Meier has joined us to talk about the flu season. Dr. Meier, the real flu season **hasn't arrived yet,** but we**'ve already heard** about a number of serious cases.

DR. MEIER: Yes. As this chart shows, it *is* early for so many cases.

TOM: I got my shot two weeks ago. **Has** it **started** to work **yet?**

DR. MEIER: **Yes,** it **has.** It starts working in about a week.

TOM: See that guy over at the sports desk? That's our sportscaster, Randy Marlow. Hey Randy, **have** you **gotten** your flu shot **yet?**

RANDY: **Not yet!**

TOM: Randy's afraid of needles. I think he'd rather catch the flu.

DR. MEIER: Well, our lab is testing bananas that can produce vaccines.

TOM: No more needles! **Have** they **started** to sell them **yet?**

DR. MEIER: **No,** they **haven't.** But . . .

TOM: Oops! We**'ve already run out** of time. Thanks, Dr. Meier.

GRAMMAR **PRESENTATION**
PRESENT PERFECT: *ALREADY* AND *YET*

			PAST PARTICIPLE OF VERB	
SUBJECT	*HAVE / HAS*	*ALREADY*		
They	**have**	*already*	**developed**	a new flu vaccine.
It	**has**		**saved**	many lives.

AFFIRMATIVE STATEMENTS: *ALREADY*

SUBJECT	*HAVE NOT / HAS NOT*	PAST PARTICIPLE OF VERB		*YET*
They	**haven't**	**finished**	the interview	*yet*.
It	**hasn't**	**ended**		

NEGATIVE STATEMENTS: *YET*

HAVE / HAS	SUBJECT	PAST PARTICIPLE OF VERB		*YET*
Have	they	**tested**	the new vaccine	*yet*?
Has	it	**gotten**	approval	

YES / NO QUESTIONS: *YET*

SHORT ANSWERS

	AFFIRMATIVE
Yes,	they **have**.
	it **has**.

SHORT ANSWERS

	NEGATIVE
No,	they **haven't**.
	it **hasn't**.
No, not yet.	

NOTES

EXAMPLES

1. We often use the **present perfect** with *already* in affirmative sentences to talk about events that happened some time <u>before now</u>. It is possible that the event happened earlier than expected.

A: Is your daughter going to get her flu shot?

B: She**'s** *already* **gotten** it.

▶ **BE CAREFUL!** Do not use the present perfect with *already* when you mention a specific past point in time or a past time expression.

DON'T SAY: ~~She's already gotten it last month.~~

Already usually comes between *have / has* and the past participle.

• Researchers **have** *already* **discovered** cures for many diseases.

Already can also come at the end of the clause.

• They**'ve made** a lot of progress *already*.

2. Use the **present perfect** with *not yet* to talk about events that have not happened <u>before now</u>. It is possible that we expected the event to have happened earlier, and it is still possible that the event will happen in the future.

• They **haven't discovered** a cure for the common cold *yet*, but they hope to discover one in the future.

Notice that *yet* usually comes at the end of the clause.

• The flu season **hasn't arrived** *yet*.

Yet can also come between *have not / has not* and the past participle.

• They **haven't** *yet* **discovered** a cure for the common cold.

3. We usually use *yet* **in questions** to find out if something has happened <u>before now</u>.

• **Has** your son **gotten** his flu shot *yet*?

USAGE NOTE: Sometimes we use *already* **in a question** to express surprise that something happened sooner than expected.

• **Has** he *already* **gotten** his flu shot? The flu season hasn't begun yet.

FOCUSED PRACTICE

① DISCOVER THE GRAMMAR

Match the cause with the result.

Cause	Result
__e__ **1.** Tom has already gotten his flu shot, so he probably	**a.** is really hungry.
_____ **2.** Dr. Meier has already finished his interview, so he	**b.** may get the flu.
_____ **3.** Dr. Meier hasn't had lunch yet, so he	**c.** has left the TV studio.
_____ **4.** Randy hasn't gotten his shot yet, so he	**d.** isn't very hungry.
_____ **5.** Randy has already had lunch, so he	**e.** won't get the flu this year.

② ASK DR. MEIER Grammar Notes 1–3

*Complete these questions and answers from a magazine article. Use the present perfect form of the verbs in parentheses with **already** or **yet** and short answers.*

smallpox vaccine	tetanus vaccine	flu vaccine	polio vaccine	measles vaccine	world smallpox vaccination program	last case of smallpox	AIDS vaccine	cancer vaccine	malaria vaccine	common cold vaccine
1796	1880	1945	1954	1963	1966	1980	NOW			

Q: We plan to travel to the rain forest next year. _____Have_____ they _____found_____ a
    1. (find)

   malaria vaccine _____yet_____?

A: _____, they _____. Talk to your doctor about ways to prevent this
                                2.

   disease.

Q: My doctor told me I won't need another smallpox vaccination. I was surprised.

   _____ smallpox completely _____?
                                3. (disappear)

A: _____, it _____.
                       4.

Q: They _____ vaccines against the flu. What about the common cold?
           5. (develop)

A: No. Because there are so many different cold viruses, they _____ to develop
                                                              6. (be able)

   a vaccine _____.

Q: There has been so much cancer research. _____ anyone _____ a
                                                                7. (make)

   successful vaccine _____?

A: _____, they _____. Researchers *have* made a lot of progress in
                       8.

   recent years, however.

3 MEDICAL RECORD

Look at Rita's immunization chart. Use the words in parentheses to write statements with the present perfect and **already** *or* **yet**.

LIFETIME IMMUNIZATIONS						
NAME: Rita Meier						
		(2 mos.)	(4 mos.)	(6 mos.)	(15–18 mos.)	(4–6 yrs.)
		Date Given	Date Given	Date Given	Date Given	Date Given
D P T	Diphtheria Pertussis Tetanus	12/14/98	2/2/99	4/16/99		
P O L I O		12/14/98	2/2/99	4/16/99		

(12–15 mos.)		Date Given	Date Given	(18–24 mos.)		Date Given
M M R	Measles Mumps Rubella	10/19/99		H I B	Hemophilus Influenzae Type B	
(Booster every 10 yrs.)			Date	Date		Date
Tetanus Diphtheria						

1. (The Meiers / take Rita to the doctor)

The Meiers have already taken Rita to the doctor.

2. (The doctor / give Rita her 15–18 month DPT injection)

The doctor hasn't given Rita her 15–18 month DPT injection yet.

3. (Rita / get her 6-month DPT injection)

_____

4. (Rita / receive / her 15–18 month polio immunization)

_____

5. (Rita / be to the doctor for her MMR immunization)

_____

6. (She / get a tetanus booster)

_____

7. (The doctor / vaccinate Rita against the mumps)

_____

8. (Rita / receive / an HIB vaccine)

_____

COMMUNICATION PRACTICE

4 LISTENING

Dr. Meier is speaking to his wife, Gisela. Listen to their conversation. Listen again and check the things that Dr. Meier has already done.

Monday, October 2
- ☑ A.M. America Interview
- ☐ Appointment with
  Dr. Bellini—flu shot
- ☐ Go to lab
- ☐ Mail rent check
- ☐ Pick up film
- ☐ Read article about
  banana vaccine

5 INFORMATION GAP: CHORES

Work in pairs (A and B). Student B, look at the Information Gap on p. 183 and follow the instructions there. Student A, look at the picture of the Meiers' dining room on this page. Cross out the chores Gisela has already done. Ask your partner about Helmut's chores and cross out the chores he's already done. Answer your partner's questions about Gisela's chores.

EXAMPLE:

A: Has Helmut bought film yet?

B: Yes, he has. OR Yes, he's already bought film.
Has Gisela vacuumed the carpet yet?

A: No, she hasn't. OR No, not yet.

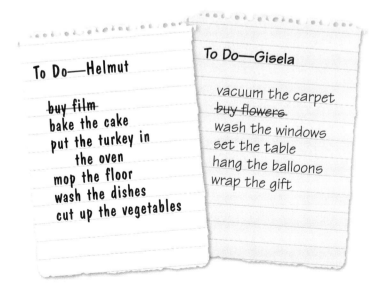

To Do—Helmut

buy film
bake the cake
put the turkey in
the oven
mop the floor
wash the dishes
cut up the vegetables

To Do—Gisela

vacuum the carpet
buy flowers
wash the windows
set the table
hang the balloons
wrap the gift

Now compare lists with your partner. Are they the same?

6 WHAT ABOUT YOU?

Write a list of things that you planned or wanted to do by this time (for example: find a new job, paint the apartment). Include things that you have already done and things that you haven't done yet. Exchange lists with a classmate, and ask and answer questions about the items on the lists.

EXAMPLE:

A: Have you found a new job yet?

B: No, not yet. I'm still looking. OR Yes, I have.

7 INVENTIONS AND DISCOVERIES

Work in pairs. Decide together if the following things have already happened or have not happened yet. Check the appropriate column. Discuss your answers with your classmates.

EXAMPLE:

A: Researchers haven't discovered a cure for the common cold yet.

B: They've already found a test for the virus that causes AIDS, but they haven't found a cure yet.

	Already	Not Yet
1. a cure for the common cold	☐	☑
2. a test for the AIDS virus	☑	☐
3. a successful heart transplant (animal to human)	☐	☐
4. a successful heart transplant (human to human)	☐	☐
5. a cure for tooth decay (cavities)	☐	☐
6. a pillow that helps prevent snoring	☐	☐
7. liquid sunglasses (in the form of eye drops)	☐	☐
8. electric cars	☐	☐
9. flying cars	☐	☐
10. light bulbs that can last ten years	☐	☐

Add your own list of inventions and discoveries.

	Already	Not Yet
11. _____	☐	☐
12. _____	☐	☐
13. _____	☐	☐

8 WRITING

Imagine you and a friend are giving a party tonight. Leave a note for your friend to explain what you've already done and what you haven't done yet.

> **EXAMPLE:**
>
> I've already bought the soda, but I haven't gotten the potato chips yet . . .

INFORMATION GAP FOR STUDENT B

Student B, look at the Meiers' kitchen. Cross out the chores Helmut has already done. Answer your partner's questions about Helmut's chores. Ask your partner about Gisela's chores and cross out the chores she's already done.

> **EXAMPLE:**
>
> **A:** Has Helmut bought film yet?
>
> **B:** Yes, he has. OR Yes, he's already bought film.
>   Has Gisela vacuumed the carpet yet?
>
> **A:** No, she hasn't. OR No, not yet.

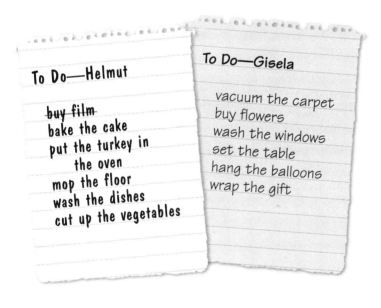

To Do—Helmut

~~buy film~~
bake the cake
put the turkey in
   the oven
mop the floor
wash the dishes
cut up the vegetables

To Do—Gisela

vacuum the carpet
buy flowers
wash the windows
set the table
hang the balloons
wrap the gift

Now compare lists with your partner. Are they the same?

PRESENT PERFECT: INDEFINITE PAST

GRAMMAR **IN CONTEXT**

BEFORE YOU READ What kind of a TV show is "Feldstein"? Where can you find a message like this?

Read this online journal message from TV star Jimmy Feldstein to fans of his show, "Feldstein."

XYZ TV CENTRAL ONLINE

XYZ TV Central | **Feldstein**

SEARCH · CHAT · E-MAIL · JIMMY'S JOURNAL · TICKETS

Jimmy's Journal 11/17/00

Hello again from Los Angeles! As you know, I**'ve just won** the Emmy Award for Best Actor in a TV comedy series. The whole cast **has come** along for the award ceremonies.

We love L.A., but the weather! Today there's a 90% chance of rain and an 80% chance that your hair gel will melt. Who**'s ever heard** of a weather forecast like that?

Thanks for all your e-mail. A lot of you **have asked** me: "**Have** you **ever had** any doubts about your success?" Of course, I **have**. I**'ve been** on every talk show at least twice and my face **has appeared** on the cover of three major magazines, but I still can't believe this is really happening to me!

So, what's next? Well, the show's been on for two years, and we**'ve** all **just signed** a contract for two more. But I want to do more. I**'ve never acted** in a play, for example. Hey guys, **have** you **read** any good scripts **lately?**

Oh, one more thing—I**'ve recently signed** a contract to write a book about relationships. Be honest. How many times **have** you **gone** on a date just because you didn't feel like cooking? I**'ve done** that! Well, this will be a book for people like me.

See you back in New York next week. Until then, keep laughing!

Jimmy

GRAMMAR **PRESENTATION**
PRESENT PERFECT: INDEFINITE PAST

STATEMENTS

SUBJECT	HAVE / HAS (NOT)	PAST PARTICIPLE OF VERB	
They	**have (not)**	**appeared** **been**	on TV.
It	**has (not)**		

See page 167 in Unit 16 for a complete presentation of present perfect forms.

STATEMENTS WITH ADVERBS

SUBJECT	HAVE / HAS	ADVERB	PAST PARTICIPLE OF VERB		ADVERB
They	**have**	*never* *just* *recently*	**appeared** **been**	on TV.	
It	**has**				
They	**have (not)**		**appeared** **been**	on TV	*lately*. *recently*.
It	**has (not)**				

YES / NO QUESTIONS

HAVE / HAS	SUBJECT	(EVER)	PAST PARTICIPLE OF VERB	
Have	they	*(ever)*	**appeared** **been**	on TV?
Has	it			

SHORT ANSWERS

AFFIRMATIVE	
Yes,	they **have.**
	it **has.**

SHORT ANSWERS

NEGATIVE	
No,	they **haven't.**
	it **hasn't.**
No, *never*.	

WH- QUESTIONS

WH- WORD	HAVE / HAS	SUBJECT	PAST PARTICIPLE OF VERB	
How often	**have**	they	**appeared** **been**	on TV?
	has	it		

NOTES	EXAMPLES

1. Use the **present perfect** to talk about things that happened at an <u>indefinite time in the past</u>. You can use the present perfect when you don't know when something happened, when you do not want to be specific, or when the specific time is not important.

- They**'ve won** several awards.
- I**'ve interviewed** the whole cast.
- She**'s been** in a Hollywood movie.

2. Use the **present perfect** to talk about <u>repeated actions</u> at some indefinite time in the past.

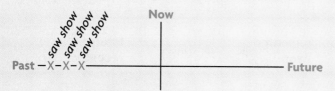

- He**'s been** on a lot of talk shows over the past two weeks.
- I**'ve seen** his show many times.

3. You can use *ever* with the **present perfect** to <u>ask questions</u>. It means *at any time up until the present*.

Use *never* to answer <u>negatively</u>.

A: **Have** you **won** an award?
　　　　　　OR
　　Have you *ever* **won** an award?

B: No, I've *never* **won** one.
　　　　OR
　　No, *never*.

4. Use the **present perfect** with certain **adverbs of time** to emphasize that something happened in the <u>very recent</u> (but still indefinite) <u>past</u>.

USAGE NOTE: In spoken American English people often use *just* and *recently* with the <u>simple past tense</u> to refer to indefinite time.

- We've *just* **gotten** back from LA.
- I've *recently* **signed** a contract to write a book.
- He **hasn't had** time *lately*.

- We *just* **got** back from LA.

FOCUSED PRACTICE

1 DISCOVER THE GRAMMAR

Read the first sentence. Then decide if the second sentence is **True (T)** *or* **False (F)**.

1. I've recently joined the show.
<u>T</u>   I am a new cast member.

2. I have never been to Los Angeles.
_____   I went to Los Angeles a long time ago.

3. I've just finished Jimmy's book.
_____   I finished it a little while ago.

4. Greg asks, "Have you ever seen this movie?"
_____   Greg wants to know when you saw the movie.

5. Arlene asks you, "Have you read any good books lately?"
_____   Arlene wants to know about a book you read last year.

6. She's visited New York several times.
_____   This is her first visit to New York.

7. She has become very popular.
_____   She is popular now.

2 BLIND DATE

In this scene from "Feldstein," Jimmy and Ursula are on a blind date—they have never met before. Complete the sentences using the present perfect form of the verbs in the box. Some verbs are used more than once.

have	make	stop	talk	travel	want

URSULA: This is a nice restaurant. _____Have_____ you _____had_____ their steak?
                                                      1.

JIMMY: No, but I _____ the eggplant parmigiana. In fact, I always have that.
                    2.

URSULA: Then try some of my steak tonight.

JIMMY: Actually, I _____ eating meat.
                     3.

URSULA: Oh, really? Are you a Save the Animals person?

JIMMY: Oh, no. It's not that I love animals. I just hate plants. _____ you ever

really _____ to a plant? They have absolutely nothing to say.
                    4.

URSULA: Right. So, _____ you ever _____ to live outside of

New York?
                                                            5.

(continued on next page)

JIMMY: Outside of New York? Where's that? But seriously, I _____ never

_____ to try any other place. I love it here.
6.

URSULA: But _____ you ever _____ to a different city?
7.

JIMMY: Why should I do that? No, traveling is definitely not for me. You like it here

too, right?

URSULA: It's OK, but I _____ to other places too. It's a big world out there.
8.

JIMMY: I like it right here. Say, _____ you _____ plans
9.

for tomorrow night? How about dinner? Same time, same place, same

eggplant parmigiana . . .

---

3 BRAINSTORMING Grammar Note 3

*Two writers are brainstorming story ideas for Jimmy's show. They want to do
something different, so they are trying to remember what they have done in past
shows. Use the words in parentheses to write questions and answers. Use **ever**
with the questions and, when appropriate, use **never** with the answers.*

1. **A:** (we / do / a story about a blind date?)

   Have we ever done a story about a blind date?

   B: Yes, _____we have_____. Jimmy went out with Ursula, remember?

2. **A:** Oh, yeah. Well, here's another idea.

   (Greg's parents / stay / in his apartment?)

   _____

   B: No, _____. But they've been on the show recently.

3. **A:** OK. Then we need something with Gizmo.

   (Gizmo / look for / a job?)

   _____

   B: No, _____. That might be funny. Gizmo finds a job, and his new

   boss sends him on a trip. Maybe to Europe.

4. A: That sounds familiar.

(the characters / travel / to Europe?)

_____

B: Yes, _____, but not recently. Arlene went to Spain last year.

5. A: So let's develop this one.

(Gizmo / take / a plane?)

_____

B: No, _____. This can be his first flight.

6. A: Good. That will get lots of laughs.

(he / study / a foreign language?)

_____

B: Yes, _____. When he fell in love with the Italian tour guide.

7. A: So he goes to Rome, and he *thinks* he understands everything.

(you / write / anything like this?)

_____

B: No, _____. I'd better buy an Italian dictionary.

④ EDITING

Read this message from Jimmy Feldstein's online message board. Find and correct five mistakes in the use of the present perfect. The first mistake is already corrected.

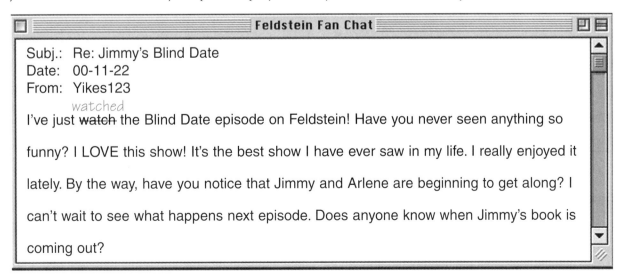

Subj.: Re: Jimmy's Blind Date
Date: 00-11-22
From: Yikes123

I've just ~~watch~~ *watched* the Blind Date episode on Feldstein! Have you never seen anything so funny? I LOVE this show! It's the best show I have ever saw in my life. I really enjoyed it lately. By the way, have you notice that Jimmy and Arlene are beginning to get along? I can't wait to see what happens next episode. Does anyone know when Jimmy's book is coming out?

5 ONLINE WITH GIZMO

Complete the XYZ Network online interview with Jake Stewart, the actor who plays the part of Gizmo on Jimmy's show.

XYZ TV'S LIVE STUDIO

XYZ online LIVE STUDIO Feldstein

ONLINE INTERVIEW WITH JAKE STEWART OF XYZ'S FELDSTEIN

XYZ:

Welcome to Live Studio, Jake. Your character, Gizmo, has become famous.

How many online interviews have you done?
1. (How many / online interviews / do?)

JAKE:

None! _____ Very exciting!
2. (Never even / be / in a chat room)

XYZ:

You used to do stand-up comedy. _____ on TV?
3. (How / change / as an actor)

JAKE:

I work with a group, so _____
4. (become / a better team player / lately)

XYZ:

As a comic actor, _____
5. (who / be / your role model?)

JAKE:

Hard to say. _____
6. (Charlie Chaplin / have / a great influence on me)

XYZ:

Yes, I can see that. _____
7. (What / be / your best moment on Jimmy's show?)

JAKE:

_____ That was a great moment for all of us.
8. (Jimmy / just / win / the Emmy)

XYZ:

All in all, _____
9. (what / enjoy / the most about this experience?)

JAKE:

Free coffee! No, really, _____
10. (meet / some fantastic people on this show)

6 ALL IN A DAY'S WORK

Look at some of Jimmy's things. Write statements using the present perfect form of the verbs in the box.

~~be~~	meet	perform	see	win	write

1. _____ He's been on three _____

         magazine covers.

2. _____

_____

3. _____

_____

4. _____

_____

5. _____

_____

6. _____

_____

COMMUNICATION PRACTICE

7 LISTENING

Lynette Long is a TV star. She is talking to her travel agent about different vacation possibilities. The travel agent is asking questions about where she has traveled before. Read the choices that follow. Listen to their conversation. Then listen again and check the travel package her agent is going to offer her.

_____ **a.** Switzerland—$1,220 includes: round-trip ticket, five nights in a beautiful hotel, day trips in the mountains, fresh air, and lots of exercise

_____ **b.** Jamaica—$600 includes: round-trip ticket, six days and five nights in a beautiful hotel, all meals, lots of beaches

_____ **c.** Egypt—$2,500 group tour includes: eight days and seven nights, beautiful hotel, all meals, bus tours to the pyramids

8 HAVE YOU EVER?

*Ask your classmates questions. Find out how many people have ever done any of the following things. If the answer is **yes**, ask more questions. Get the stories behind the answers. Share your answers and stories with the class.*

- Meet a famous TV or movie star
- Take a long trip by car
- Climb a mountain

- Dream in a foreign language
- Walk in the rain
- Drive cross-country

Add your own:

- _____

- _____

> **EXAMPLE:**
> **A:** Have you ever met a famous movie star?
> **B:** Yes, I have. I was visiting Hollywood, and I saw . . .

9 WRITING

*Write a paragraph about a character on a TV show that you watch regularly. What has the show been like lately? Has the character changed recently? Use the present perfect with **lately**, **recently**, and **never**.*

> **EXAMPLE:**
> I watch "Frasier" every Thursday night. Recently, the show has been funnier than usual . . .

PRESENT PERFECT AND SIMPLE PAST TENSE

GRAMMAR **IN CONTEXT**

BEFORE YOU READ What do you think a "commuter marriage" is? What is happening in the cartoon? How do you think the people feel?

Read this excerpt from an article in Modern Day *magazine.*

◆ LIFESTYLES ◆

Commuter Marriages

Many modern marriages are finding interesting solutions to difficult problems. Take Joe and Maria Tresante, for example. Joe and Maria **married** in June 1995. They **lived** in Detroit for three years. Then in 1998 Joe, a college professor, **got** a great job offer in Los Angeles. At the same time Maria's company **moved** to Boston. They are still married, but they **have lived** apart ever since. They **have decided** to travel back and forth between Boston and Los Angeles until one of them finds a different job. Sociologists call this kind of marriage a "commuter marriage." "It **hasn't been** easy," says Maria. "Last month I **saw** Joe three times, but this month I've only **seen** him once."

It also **hasn't been** inexpensive. In addition to the cost of frequent air flights, their phone bills **have been** sky high. December's bill **was** almost $400. This month, they**'ve started** to communicate by e-mail with the hope of lowering their expenses. Is all this trouble and expense worth it? "Yes," says the couple. "It **was** a difficult decision, but so far it **has worked out** for us. It's better for both of us to have jobs that we like." The Tresantes **have had to** work hard to make their marriage succeed, but the effort **has paid off.** Joe notes, "We've been geographically separated, but we**'ve grown** a lot closer emotionally."

GRAMMAR **PRESENTATION**
PRESENT PERFECT AND SIMPLE PAST TENSE

PRESENT PERFECT
She **has been** here since 1980.
They**'ve lived** here for twenty years.
We**'ve spoken** once today.
He **hasn't flown** this month.
Has she **called** him today?

SIMPLE PAST TENSE
She **was** in Caracas in 1975.
They **lived** there for ten years.
We **spoke** twice yesterday.
She **didn't fly** last month.
Did she **call** him yesterday?

NOTES

EXAMPLES

1. The **present perfect** is used to talk about things that started in the past, <u>continue up to the present</u>, and may continue into the future.

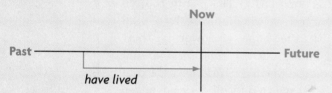

- They **have lived** apart for the past three years.
  (They started living apart three years ago and are still living apart.)

The **simple past tense** is used to talk about things that happened in the past and have <u>no connection to the present</u>.

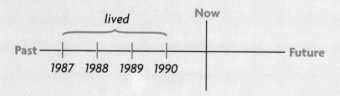

- They **lived** in Detroit for three years.
  (They lived in Detroit until 1990. They no longer live in Detroit.)

2. The **present perfect** is also used to talk about things that happened at an <u>unspecified</u> time in the past.

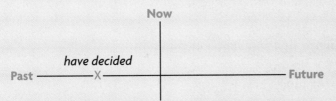

The **simple past tense** is used to talk about things that happened at a <u>specific</u> time in the past. The exact time is known and sometimes stated.

▶ **BE CAREFUL!** Do not use specific past time expressions with the present perfect except after *since*.

- They **have decided** to travel back and forth.
  (We don't know exactly when the decision was made, or the timing of the decision is not important.)

- They **lived** in Detroit *in 1990*.

- I **lived** in Detroit in 1997.
  NOT ~~I've lived in Detroit in 1997.~~

---

3. Use the **present perfect** to talk about things that have happened in a time period that is <u>not finished</u>, such as *today, this morning, this month, this year.*

Use the **simple past tense** to talk about things that happened in a time period that is <u>finished</u>, such as *yesterday, last month, last year.*

▶ **BE CAREFUL!** Some time expressions like *this morning, this month,* or *this year* can refer to a finished or unfinished time period. Use the present perfect if the time period is unfinished. Use the simple past tense if the time period is finished.

- She**'s had** three cups of coffee *this morning.*
  (It's still this morning, and it's possible that she will have some more.)

- She **had** three cups of coffee *yesterday.*
  (Yesterday is finished.)

- It's 10:00 A.M. She**'s had** three cups of coffee *this morning.*
  (The morning is not over.)

- It's 1:00 P.M. She **had** three cups of coffee *this morning.*
  (The morning is over.)

FOCUSED PRACTICE

1 DISCOVER THE GRAMMAR

Read the information about Joe and Maria. Then circle the letter of the sentence
*(**a** or **b**) that best describes the situation.*

1. It's 1999. Joe's family moved to Houston in 1989. They still live there.
   a. Joe's family lived in Houston for ten years.
   b. Joe's family has lived in Houston for ten years.

2. Last year Joe and Maria enjoyed their vacation in Canada.
   a. They had a good time.
   b. They've had a good time.

3. Joe is telling his friend about his wife, Maria.
   a. His friend asks, "How long were you married?"
   b. His friend asks, "How long have you been married?"

4. Joe is telling Maria that the weather in Los Angeles has been cloudy and hot for the past five days.
   a. Five days ago the weather started to be cloudy and hot, and it is still that way.
   b. Sometime in the past year the weather was cloudy and hot for five days.

5. Joe studied the piano for ten years, but he doesn't play anymore.
   a. Joe has played the piano for ten years.
   b. Joe played the piano for ten years.

6. Maria wants to move to Los Angeles from Boston but must find a job first. She is interviewing for a job in Los Angeles.
   a. She says, "I lived in Boston for two years."
   b. She says, "I've lived in Boston for two years."

7. This month Maria and Joe have met once in Boston and once in Los Angeles and will meet once more in New York.
   a. They've seen each other twice.
   b. They saw each other twice.

2 IT HASN'T BEEN EASY   Grammar Notes 1–3

Circle the correct verb forms to complete this entry in Maria's journal.

Thursday, September 28

It's 8:00 P.M. It has been / was a hard day, and it's not over yet! I still have to work on that report.
                 1.

I've begun / began it last night, but so far I've written / wrote only two pages. And it's due tomorrow!
      2.   *3.*

Work has been / was so difficult lately. I've worked / worked late every night this week. I feel exhausted
      4.   *5.*

and I haven't gotten / didn't get much sleep last night. And, of course, I miss Joe. Even though
         6.

I've seen / saw him last week, it seems like a long time ago. Oh, there's the phone—
   7.

3 PHONE CONVERSATION

Use the words in parentheses to complete the phone conversation between Maria and Joe. Use the present perfect or the simple past tense.

JOE: Hi, honey! How are you?

MARIA: I'm OK—a little tired, I guess. I only _____slept_____ a few hours last night.
1. (sleep)

I'm writing this big report for tomorrow's meeting, and I _____
2. (not stop)

worrying about it all week.

JOE: You need to rest. Listen—maybe I'll come see you this weekend. We

_____ each other twice this month.
3. (only see)

MARIA: OK. But I really have to work. Remember the last time you _____
4. (come)

here? I _____ any work at all.
5. (not do)

JOE: OK. Now, why don't you go make yourself a cup of coffee and just relax?

MARIA: Coffee! You must be kidding! I _____ five cups today. And
6. (already have)

yesterday I _____ at least six. No more coffee for me.
7. (drink)

JOE: Well then, get some rest, and I'll see you tomorrow.

MARIA: OK. Good night!

4 AN INTERVIEW

Read the magazine article on page 193 again. Imagine that you wrote the article. You asked Joe and Maria questions to get your information. What were they? Use the words below and write the questions.

1. How long / be married?

   How long have you been married?

2. How long / have your job?

   _____

3. How long / live in Detroit?

   _____

4. When / get a job offer?

   _____

(continued on next page)

5. When / your company move?

_____

6. How long / live apart?

_____

7. How often / see each other last month?

_____

8. How often / see each other this month?

_____

5 **CHANGES**

Joe and Maria met in the 1980s. Since then Joe has changed. Use the words below and write down how Joe has changed.

In the 1980s	Since then
1. have / long hair	become / bald
2. be / clean shaven	grow / a beard
3. be / thin	get / heavy
4. be / a student	become / a professor
5. live / in a dormitory	buy / a house
6. be / single	get / married

1. ___In the 1980s Joe had long hair.___

___Since then, he has become bald.___

2. In the 1980s _____

Since then, _____

3. _____

_____

4. _____

_____

5. _____

_____

6. _____

_____

COMMUNICATION PRACTICE

6 LISTENING

A school newspaper is interviewing two college professors. Listen to the interview. Then listen again and check the items that are now true.

The professors . . .

☑ **1.** are married   ☐ **2.** live in different cities   ☐ **3.** are at the same university

☐ **4.** live in Boston   ☐ **5.** are in Austin   ☐ **6.** have a house

7 MARRIAGE AND DIVORCE

Look at the chart. Work in pairs and discuss the marriage and divorce statistics in the United States. Use the words in the box.

↑ increase	decrease
get higher	get lower
go up	↓ go down

	1980	1990	1995
Marriage	2,406,708	2,948,000	2,336,000
Divorce	1,189,000	1,175,000	1,169,000
Percentage of men (age 20–24) never married	68.8%	79.7%	80.7%
Percentage of women (age 20–24) never married	50.2%	64.1%	66.7%
Average age of first marriage: men **women**	24.7 22.0	26.1 23.9	26.9 24.5

Source: Department of Commerce, Bureau of the Census and the Department of Health and Human Services, National Center for Health Statistics.

> EXAMPLE:
> The number of marriages has decreased since 1980.
> In 1980 a total of 2,406,708 people got married.
> In 1995 2,336,000 got married.

8 A COUNTRY YOU KNOW WELL

Work in small groups. Tell your classmates about some changes in a country you know well.

> EXAMPLE:
> In 1999, a new president took office. Since then, the economy has improved.

9 LOOKING BACK

Work in pairs. Look at Maria's records from last year and this year. It's now the beginning of August. Compare what Maria did last year with what she's done this year.

LAST YEAR					
January	**February**	**March**	**April**	**May**	**June**
• business trip to N.Y. • L.A.—2X	• L.A.—2X • 1 seminar	• business trip to N.Y. • L.A.—1X	• L.A.—3X • 1 lecture	• 10 vacation days • Jay's wedding	• 2 seminars • L.A.—2X
July	**August**	**September**	**October**	**November**	**December**
• L.A.—1X • Sue's wedding	• L.A.—1X	• L.A.—2X • 1 lecture	• business trip to Little Rock	• 1 seminar	• 10 vacation days
THIS YEAR					
January	**February**	**March**	**April**	**May**	**June**
• L.A.—1X	• business trip to N.Y • 1 lecture	• L.A.—1X • Nan's wedding	• L.A.—1X	• business trip to Miami • L.A.—1X	• 5 vacation days • 1 seminar
July	**August**	**September**	**October**	**November**	**December**
• Barry's wedding	• L.A.—1X • 1 lecture				

EXAMPLE:

A: Last year she went on three business trips.

B: So far this year she's only gone on two.

10 WRITING

How has your family changed in the last five years? Write a paragraph about some of the changes. Use the present perfect and the simple past tense.

EXAMPLE:

Five years ago, all my brothers and sisters lived at home. Since then, we have all moved away . . .

PRESENT PERFECT PROGRESSIVE

GRAMMAR **IN CONTEXT**

BEFORE YOU READ   Look at the photo. What can you guess about the man? Where is he? Look at the statistics at the end of the article. In which categories do you think the man belongs?

A journalist has been writing a series of articles about the problem of homelessness in the United States. Read this second in a series of five articles.

LIVING ON THE STREETS
Part two in a five-part series

BY ENRICO SANCHEZ

It **has been raining.** The ground is still wet. John Tarver **has been sitting** on the same park bench for hours. His clothes are soaked and he **has been coughing** all morning. A while ago someone gave him a bowl of hot soup. It's no longer warm, but John **has been eating** it anyway.

How did he end up like this? John, a former building superintendent, lost his job and his apartment when he hurt his back. He **has been living** on the street since then. And he is not alone. John is just one of a possible seven million Americans who **have been making** their homes in the streets, parks, and subway stations of our cities. The number of homeless men, women, and children **has been climbing** steadily since 1980 and will continue to rise until the government takes action.

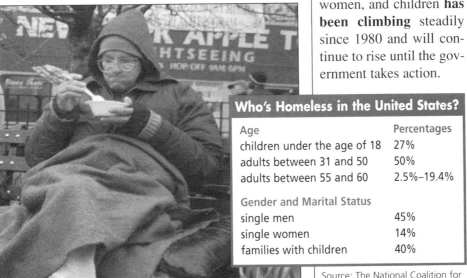

Who's Homeless in the United States?

Age	Percentages
children under the age of 18	27%
adults between 31 and 50	50%
adults between 55 and 60	2.5%–19.4%
Gender and Marital Status	
single men	45%
single women	14%
families with children	40%

Source: The National Coalition for the Homeless

GRAMMAR **PRESENTATION**
PRESENT PERFECT PROGRESSIVE

STATEMENTS

SUBJECT	HAVE / HAS (NOT)	BEEN	BASE FORM OF VERB + -ING		(SINCE / FOR)
I You* We They	**have (not)**	**been**	**sitting**	here	(**since** 12:00). (**for** hours).
He She It	**has (not)**				

YES / NO QUESTIONS

HAVE / HAS	SUBJECT	BEEN	BASE FORM OF VERB + -ING		(SINCE / FOR)
Have	I you* we they	**been**	**sitting**	here	(**since** 12:00)? (**for** an hour)?
Has	he she it				

SHORT ANSWERS

AFFIRMATIVE		
Yes,	you I / we you they	**have.**
	he she it	**has.**

SHORT ANSWERS

NEGATIVE		
No,	you I / we you they	**haven't.**
	he she it	**hasn't.**

WH- QUESTIONS

WH- WORD	HAVE / HAS	SUBJECT	BEEN	BASE FORM OF VERB + -ING	
How long	**have**	I you* we they	**been**	**sitting**	here?
	has	he she it			

SHORT ANSWERS

Since 9:00.
For a few hours.

*You is both singular and plural.

NOTES	**EXAMPLES**

1. Use the **present perfect progressive** (also called the present perfect continuous) to talk about an action or situation that <u>began in the past and continues to the present</u>. The action or situation is usually not finished. It is continuing, and it will probably continue into the future.

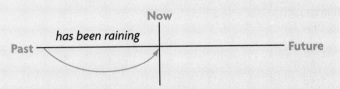

REMEMBER: <u>Non-action (stative) verbs</u> are not usually used with the progressive. *(See page 5 and Appendix 2, page A-2.)*

- It**'s been raining** all day. When is it going to stop?
- They**'ve been looking** for work, but they haven't found anything yet.
- I**'ve been reading** an interesting book. I'll give it to you when I'm finished.

- He's known a lot of homeless people.
  NOT ~~He's been knowing a lot of homeless people.~~

2. Also use the **present perfect progressive** for <u>repeated actions</u> that <u>started in the past and continue up to the present</u>. Verbs that are frequently used in this way are: *hit, punch, knock, cough, jump, nod,* and *kick.*

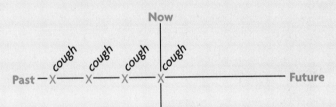

- John **has been coughing** all morning.
- The interviewer **has been nodding** his head sympathetically.
- I**'ve been knocking** on the door for two minutes. I don't think anyone is home.

3. Use the **present perfect progressive** to describe actions that have <u>stopped in the recent past</u>. The action is not happening right now, but there are <u>results</u> of the action that you <u>can still see</u>.

- It**'s been raining**. The streets are still wet.
- John **has been fighting**. He has a black eye.

FOCUSED PRACTICE

1 DISCOVER THE GRAMMAR

Read the information about John and Enrico. Then circle the letter of the sentence (a or b) that best describes the situation.

1. John has been sitting on that park bench for hours.
   a. He is still sitting on the park bench.
   b. He is no longer sitting on the park bench.

2. John's been coughing.
   a. He coughed several times.
   b. He coughed only once.

3. John's been living on the streets for two years.
   a. He used to live on the streets.
   b. He still lives on the streets.

4. Enrico has been writing an article.
   a. The article is finished.
   b. The article isn't finished yet.

5. Enrico looks out the window and says, "It's been snowing."
   a. It is definitely still snowing.
   b. It is possible that it stopped snowing a little while ago.

6. It's been snowing since 8:00.
   a. It's still snowing.
   b. It stopped snowing a little while ago.

2 AN INTERVIEW
Grammar Notes 1–3

The newspaper interviewed John Tarver. Complete the interview. Use the present perfect progressive form of the verbs in the box.

| ask | do | eat | ~~live~~ | look | read | sleep | spend | think | worry |

INTERVIEWER: How long _____ have _____ you _____ been living _____ on the streets, Mr. Tarver?
1.

MR. TARVER: For almost two years now.

INTERVIEWER: Where do you sleep?

MR. TARVER: It's been pretty warm, so I _____ in the park. But winter will be
2.
here soon, and it'll be too cold to sleep outside. I _____ about that.
3.

INTERVIEWER: What _____ you _____ about food?
4.

MR. TARVER: I _____ much lately. Sometimes someone gives me money, and
5. (negative)
I buy a sandwich and something to drink.

INTERVIEWER: How _____ you _____ your time?

6.

MR. TARVER: I do a lot of thinking. Recently, I _____ a lot about my past and

7.

how I ended up without a home.

INTERVIEWER: Do you see any way out of your present situation?

MR. TARVER: I want to work, so I _____ for a job. I _____ the want

8.   9.

ads every day in the paper, and I _____ everyone I know for a job.

10.

INTERVIEWER: Any luck?

MR. TARVER: So far, no.

---

❸ WHAT'S BEEN HAPPENING? Grammar Notes 1–3

*Look at the two pictures of journalist Enrico Sanchez. Write sentences describing
what is going on in these two pictures. Use the present perfect progressive form of
the verbs in parentheses. Choose between affirmative and negative forms.*

1. He has been writing an article about the homeless.

(write an article about the homeless)

2. _____

(read the newspaper)

3. _____

(drink coffee)

4. _____

(drink tea)

5. _____

(eat)

6. _____

(watch TV)

7. _____

(rain)

COMMUNICATION PRACTICE

4 LISTENING

Listen to Dave, a counselor at a job training program, talk to Martha, a homeless woman. Listen again and check the things Dave is still doing. Listen a third time and check the things Martha is still doing.

Dave

☑ **1.** Reviewing Martha's test results

☐ **2.** Teaching Martha to use the fax

☐ **3.** Setting up a day care program

Martha

☐ **1.** Working with computers

☐ **2.** Writing a resume

☐ **3.** Making a list of places to send her resume

☐ **4.** Walking to her job training program

☐ **5.** Looking for business clothes

☐ **6.** Taking care of her children all day

5 JOBLESSNESS AROUND THE WORLD

Work in pairs. Look at these government statistics. Discuss them with your partner. Make sentences using the present perfect progressive. Use the words in the box below.

joblessness	the unemployment rate	unemployment	
improve / get worse	go up and down	decrease / increase	fall / rise

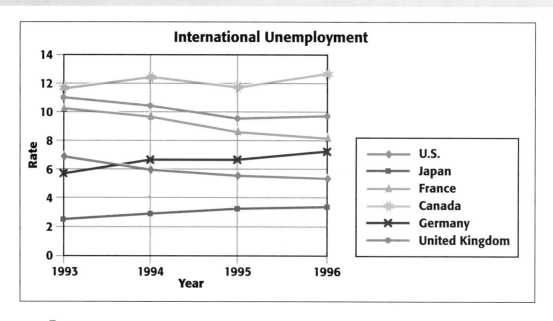

International Unemployment

EXAMPLE:

A: What's been happening in the United States?

B: The unemployment rate has been falling.

6 EXPLANATIONS

Work in pairs. Think of as many explanations as possible for the following situations.

1. John looks exhausted.
2. Martha is wearing a new suit.
3. Alexis and Tom look angry.
4. The streets are all wet.
5. Gina's wallet is stuffed with $100 bills.
6. Jason lost five pounds.

EXAMPLE:
Janet's eyes are red.
A: Maybe she's been crying.
B: Or maybe she's been suffering from allergies.
A: She's probably been rubbing them.

7 WHAT ABOUT YOU?

Complete this form with information about your present life.

address: _____

job: _____

hobbies / interests: _____

favorite school subjects: _____

plans: _____

concerns: _____

Work in pairs. Look at each other's forms. Ask and answer questions with
How long + *the present perfect progressive. The verbs in the box can help you.*

EXAMPLE:
A: How long have you been working as a cook?
B: For two years.
    OR
Since I moved here.

live at	study
work at / as	plan to
play / collect / do	worry about

8 WRITING

Write a paragraph about your present life. Use the present perfect progressive. You can use the form you filled out in Exercise 7 for ideas.

EXAMPLE:
I've been working at McDonald's for about a year. . . .

PRESENT PERFECT AND PRESENT PERFECT PROGRESSIVE

GRAMMAR **IN CONTEXT**

BEFORE YOU READ Look at the key facts about African elephants. Why do you think the elephant population has changed so much? Look at the map of Africa. What parts of Africa have elephants?

Professor Jane Owen has been studying elephants for several decades. Read this excerpt from her latest article in Science Today.

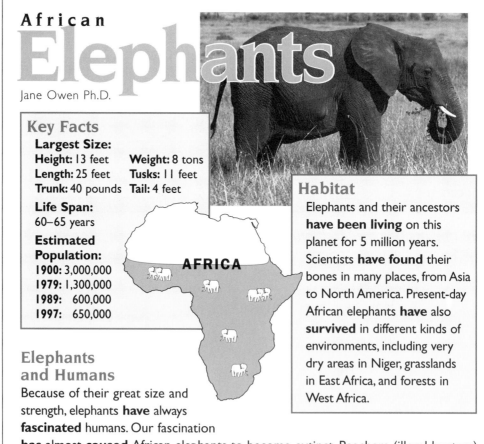

African Elephants

Jane Owen Ph.D.

Key Facts

Largest Size:
Height: 13 feet   **Weight:** 8 tons
Length: 25 feet   **Tusks:** 11 feet
Trunk: 40 pounds   **Tail:** 4 feet

Life Span:
60–65 years

Estimated Population:
1900: 3,000,000
1979: 1,300,000
1989:   600,000
1997:   650,000

AFRICA

Habitat
Elephants and their ancestors **have been living** on this planet for 5 million years. Scientists **have found** their bones in many places, from Asia to North America. Present-day African elephants **have** also **survived** in different kinds of environments, including very dry areas in Niger, grasslands in East Africa, and forests in West Africa.

Elephants and Humans
Because of their great size and strength, elephants **have** always **fascinated** humans. Our fascination **has** almost **caused** African elephants to become extinct. Poachers (illegal hunters) **have killed** hundreds of thousands of elephants for the ivory of their tusks. After 1989 it became illegal to sell ivory. Since then, the elephant population **has been growing** steadily. Recently several countries **have been protecting** elephants in national parks, and herds **have become** larger and healthier.

GRAMMAR **PRESENTATION**
PRESENT PERFECT AND PRESENT PERFECT PROGRESSIVE

PRESENT PERFECT
Elephants **have roamed** the earth for thousands of years.
I**'ve read** two books about elephants.
Dr. Owen **has written** many articles.
She**'s lived** in many countries.

PRESENT PERFECT PROGRESSIVE
Elephants **have been roaming** the earth for thousands of years.
I**'ve been reading** this book since Monday.
She**'s been writing** articles since 1990.
She**'s been living** in France for a year.

NOTES

EXAMPLES

1. The **present perfect** often shows that an activity or state is <u>finished</u>. The emphasis is on the result of the action.

The **present perfect progressive** often shows that an activity or state is <u>unfinished</u>. It started in the past and is still continuing.

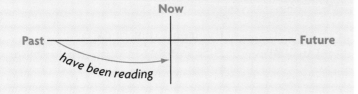

- I**'ve read** a book about elephants.
  (I finished the book.)
- She**'s written** an article.
  (She finished the article.)

- I**'ve been reading** a book about elephants.
  (I'm still reading it.)
- She**'s been writing** an article.
  (She's still writing it.)

(continued on next page)

2. Sometimes you can use either the **present perfect** OR the **present perfect progressive**. The meaning is basically the same. This is especially true when you use verbs such as *live, work, study,* and *teach* with *for* or *since*.

- She**'s studied** African elephants for three years.

  OR

- She**'s been studying** African elephants for three years.

  (In both cases, she started studying elephants three years ago, and she is still studying them.)

---

3. The **present perfect** places more emphasis on the permanence of an action or state.

The **present perfect progressive** emphasizes the temporary nature of the action.

- They**'ve** always **lived** in Africa.

- They**'ve been living** in Africa for three years, but they are returning to France next month.

---

4. We often use the **present perfect** to talk about:
  –how much someone has done
  –how many times someone has done something
  –how many things someone has done

We often use the **present perfect progressive** to talk about how long something has been happening.

▶ **BE CAREFUL!** We usually do not use the present perfect progressive when we describe a number of completed events.

- I**'ve read** a lot about it.
- I**'ve been** to Africa twice.
- She**'s written** three articles.

- I**'ve been reading** books on elephants for two months.

- I**'ve read** that book twice.
  NOT ~~I've been reading that book twice.~~

FOCUSED PRACTICE

1 DISCOVER THE GRAMMAR

*Read the first sentence. Then decide if the second sentence is **True (T)***
*or **False (F)**.*

1. Professor Owen has been reading a book about African wildlife.
  F   She finished the book.

2. She's read a book about African wildlife.
       She finished the book.

3. She's written a magazine article about the rain forest.
       She finished the article.

4. She's been waiting for some supplies.
       She received the supplies.

5. They've lived in Uganda since 1992.
       They are still in Uganda.

6. They've been living in Uganda since 1992.
       They are still in Uganda.

7. We've been discussing environmental problems with the leaders of many countries.
       The discussions are probably over.

8. We've discussed these problems with many leaders.
       The discussions are probably over.

2 PROFESSOR OWEN'S WORK   Grammar Notes 1–4

Complete these statements. Circle the correct form of the verbs. In some cases,
both forms are correct.

1. Professor Owen is working on two articles for *National Wildlife Magazine.* She

has written / (has been writing) these articles since Monday.

2. *National Wildlife Magazine* has published / has been publishing its annual report on

the environment. It is an excellent report.

3. Hundreds of African elephants have already died / have been dying this year.

4. Professor Owen has given / has been giving many talks about wildlife preservation in

past lecture series.

5. She has spoken / has been speaking at our school many times.

(continued on next page)

6. Congress <u>has created / has been creating</u> a new study group to discuss the problem of endangered animals. The group has already met twice.

7. The new group has a lot of work to do. Lately, the members <u>have studied / have been studying</u> the problem of the spotted owl.

8. Professor Owen was late for a meeting with the members of Congress. When she arrived the chairperson said, "At last, you're here. We <u>have waited / have been waiting</u> for you."

9. Professor Owen <u>has lived / has been living</u> in England for the last two years, but she will return to the United States in January.

10. She <u>has worked / has been working</u> with environmentalists in England and France.

3 GRANDAD Grammar Notes 1–4

Complete this entry from Dr. Owen's field journal. Use the present perfect or the present perfect progressive form of the verb in parentheses.

We ___'ve been hearing___ about Grandad since we arrived here in
     1. (hear)

Amboseli Park. He is one of the last "tuskers." Two days ago, we finally saw

him. His tusks are more than seven feet long. I'_____ never

_____ anything like them.
     2. (see)

Grandad _____ here for more than sixty years. He
            3. (live)

_____ everything, and he _____
     4. (experience)   **5. (survive)**

countless threats from human beings. Young men _____
                                                    6. (test)

their courage against him, and poachers _____ him for
                                          7. (hunt)

his ivory. His experience and courage _____ him so far.
                                        8. (save)

   For the last two days, he _____ slowly through the
                              9. (move)

tall grass. He _____ and _____.
                10. (eat)   **11. (rest)**

Luckily, it _____ a lot this year, and the biggest
             12. (rain)

elephants _____ enough food and water.
           13. (find)

4 **HOW LONG AND HOW MUCH?**

Professor Owen is doing fieldwork in Africa. Imagine you are about to interview her. Use the words below to ask her questions. Use her notes to complete her answers. Choose between the present perfect and present perfect progressive.

FIELD NOTES
3/23/00

GRANDAD
    Order: *Proboscidea*
    Family: *Elephantidae*
    Genus and Species: *Loxodonta africana*

—eats about 500 pounds of vegetation/day
—drinks about 40 gallons of water at a time
—walks 5 miles/hour (50 miles/day)

1. How long / you / observe / Grandad?

    YOU: How long have you been observing Grandad? _____

    OWEN: I've been observing him for _____ two days.

2. How much vegetation / he / eat?

    YOU: _____

    OWEN: _____

3. How often / he / stop for water?

    YOU: _____

    OWEN: _____ four times.

4. How much water / he / drink?

    YOU: _____

    OWEN: _____

5. How long / he / walk today?

    YOU: _____

    OWEN: _____ nine hours.

6. How far / he / travel so far today?

    YOU: _____

    OWEN: _____

COMMUNICATION PRACTICE

5 LISTENING

Listen to the conversations. Then listen again and circle the letter of the pictures that illustrate the situations.

1.

a.

b.

2.

a.

b.

3.

a.

b.

4.

a.

b.

5.

a.　　　　　　　　　　**b.**

6 GIVING ADVICE

Sometimes we are asked to give advice, but we don't have enough information. Read the following situations and list the questions you might ask to get the information you need. Work with a partner. Take turns asking and answering questions and giving advice. Try to use the present perfect or the present perfect progressive. Then role-play these situations.

1. Your friend calls you. He says that he is tired of waiting for his girlfriend. She is always late. This time he wants to leave to teach her a lesson.

Questions:
a. How long have you been waiting?
b. How often . . .
c. How many times . . .
d. Have you ever . . .

Advice: _____

2. Your father is trying to quit smoking. He's having a hard time and tells you that he needs to have just one more cigarette.

Questions:
a. How long . . .
b. How many times . . .
c. Have you ever . . .

Advice: _____

3. Your friend is an author. She has published several books and is working on a new one. She is getting very frustrated and thinks she will never finish.

Questions:
a. How many pages . . .
b. How long . . .
c. Have you ever . . .

Advice: _____

7 FIND OUT MORE

These two creatures have been on the World Wildlife Fund's list of the ten most endangered species. Do research about one of the animals.

Find out about its . . .

- size

- geographic location (habitat)

- habits

Learn . . .

- why it has become endangered

- what governments or other groups have been doing to save it

Arabian Oryx

Monarch Butterfly

Now get together in small groups and discuss your findings.

8 WRITING

Write a paragraph about one of the animals discussed in this unit. Use the topics from Exercise 7 to guide your writing.

EXAMPLE:
The Arabian oryx is about three feet tall. Its horns are . . .

REVIEW OR SELFTEST

I. *Complete the following conversations. Use the present perfect form of the verbs in parentheses.*

1. A: I've just rented a truck to move our things.

　B: _____Have_____ you ever _____driven_____ a truck before?
　　　　　　　　　　　　　　　　　　　(drive)

　A: Sure, I have. It's not that hard.

2. A: How long _____ you _____ a comedian?
　　　　　　　　　　　　　　　　　　　(be)

　B: Since I was born. I made people laugh even when I was a baby.

3. A: Shh. The baby _____ just _____ asleep.
　　　　　　　　　　　　　　　　　　　　　　　(fall)

　B: Sorry. We'll be more quiet.

4. A: It's time to pay the bills.

　B: They're not as bad as they look. I _____ already

　_____ the phone bill.
　　　(pay)

5. A: _____ you ever _____ a letter of complaint?
　　　　　　　　　　　　　　　　　(write)

　B: Yes, I have. I got great results.

6. A: Can I throw this magazine out yet?

　B: Not yet. Jennifer _____ it yet.
　　　　　　　　　　　　　(not read)

7. A: I win!

　B: I quit! You _____ every card game so far this evening.
　　　　　　　　　　　　(win)

8. A: What have you told the kids about our holiday plans?

　B: I _____ them anything yet. Let's wait until our
　　　　　(not tell)
　plans are definite.

9. A: _____ the letter carrier _____ yet?
　　　　　　　　　　　　　　　　　　(come)

　B: Yes, he has. About an hour ago. You got two letters.

10. A: Would you like some coffee?

　B: No, thanks. I _____ three cups already.
　　　　　　　　　　　(have)

II. *Complete the conversations with* **since** *or* **for***.*

    1. A: What happened? I've been waiting for you _____*since*_____ 7:00.

       B: My train broke down. I sat in the tunnel for an hour.

    2. A: How long have you lived in San Francisco?

       B: _____ I was born. How about you?

       A: I've only been here _____ a few months.

    3. A: When did you and Alan meet?

       B: I've known Alan _____ ages. We went to elementary school together.

    4. A: Has Greg worked at Cafe Fidelio for a long time?

       B: Not too long. He's only been there _____ 1998.

    5. A: Why didn't you answer the door? I've been standing here ringing the doorbell

          _____ five minutes.

       B: I didn't hear you. I was taking a shower.

    6. A: How long have you had trouble sleeping, Mr. Yang?

       B: _____ March. It started when I moved.

    7. A: Celia has been studying English _____ she was ten.

       B: That's why she speaks so well.

    8. A: Did you know that Gary plans to change jobs?

       B: He's been saying that _____ the past two years. He never does anything

         about it.

III. *Each sentence has four underlined words or phrases. The four underlined parts of the sentences are marked A, B, C, or D. Circle the letter of the <u>one</u> underlined word or phrase that is NOT CORRECT.*

    1. I<u>'ve wanted</u> to visit Hawaii <u>since</u> years, but I <u>haven't been</u> there <u>yet</u>.
          A   B   C   D
            A (**B**) **C** **A**

    2. We <u>went</u> there last year <u>after</u> we <u>have</u> <u>visited</u> Japan.
           A   B   C   D
            A **B** **C** **D**

    3. <u>Have</u> you <u>been</u> <u>living</u> in California <u>since</u> a long time?
         A   B   C   D
            A **B** **C** **D**

    4. I <u>lived</u> here <u>since</u> I <u>got</u> married <u>in</u> 1998.
          A   B   C   D
            A **B** **C** **D**

    5. We<u>'ve</u> been <u>wait</u> for Ju-yen <u>for</u> an hour, but she hasn't arrived <u>yet</u>.
         A   B   C   D
            A **B** **C** **D**

6. Todd <u>is</u> excited right now <u>because</u> he's <u>lately</u> <u>won</u> an Emmy.
       _A   _B   _C _D
                                                                                    A B C D

7. <u>It's</u> only 9:00, and <u>she already</u> <u>had</u> four cups of tea <u>this</u> morning.
    _A   _B   _C   _D
                                                                                      A B C D

8. I'<u>m watching</u> television <u>for</u> the last three <u>hours</u> and now I <u>feel</u> worried
      _A   _B   _C   _D
                                                                                 A B C D

about that test tomorrow.

9. Paz <u>been working</u> <u>for</u> Intellect <u>since</u> he <u>moved</u> to Silicon Valley.
          _A   _B   _C   _D
                                                                               A B C D

10. <u>Has he moved</u> here a long time <u>ago</u>, or <u>has</u> he just <u>arrived</u>?
       _A   _B   _C   _D
                                                                             A B C D

IV. *Circle the letter of the correct answer to complete each sentence.*

1. _____ you ever appeared on a game show, Mr. Smith?   **A B Ⓒ D**
    (A) Did   (C) Have
    (B) Has   (D) Was

2. No, but I've _____ wanted to.   **A B C D**
    (A) ever   (C) don't
    (B) yet   (D) always

3. Why _____ you decide to try out for Risk?   **A B C D**
    (A) did   (C) have
    (B) were   (D) are

4. My wife _____ your show for years now.   **A B C D**
    (A) watches   (C) was watching
    (B) is watching   (D) has been watching

5. She has always _____ I should apply as a contestant.   **A B C D**
    (A) saying   (C) said
    (B) says   (D) say

6. You're a librarian. How long _____ that kind of work?   **A B C D**
    (A) did you do   (C) do you do
    (B) have you done   (D) were you doing

7. I've been a reference librarian since _____.   **A B C D**
    (A) a long time   (C) 1990
    (B) three years   (D) I've graduated from
                                   library school

8. Have you been interested in game shows since you _____   **A B C D**
a librarian?
    (A) became   (C) become
    (B) have become   (D) have been becoming

(continued on next page)

9. I've only _____ them for about a year.　　　　　　　**A　B　C　D**

(A) watching　　　　　　　　　　(C) been watching

(B) watch　　　　　　　　　　　(D) watches

10. Have you been studying the rules for the show _____
we called?　　　　　　　　　　　　　　　　　　　　　　　　　　**A　B　C　D**

(A) for　　　　　　　　　　　　(C) since

(B) when　　　　　　　　　　　(D) as soon as

11. I _____ them for weeks, but I still don't understand them.　　**A　B　C　D**

(A) read　　　　　　　　　　　(C) was reading

(B) reading　　　　　　　　　　(D) 've been reading

V. *Complete each conversation with the correct form of the verb in parentheses.
Choose between affirmative and negative forms.*

1. (see)

A: _____Have_____ you _____seen_____ *Triassic Park* yet?
　　　　　　　　　　　　　　　　a.

B: Yes, I have. I _____ it last night. Why?
　　　　　　　　　　　b.

A: I'm seeing it on Friday. Is it good?

2. (drink)

A: Who _____ all the soda?
　　　　　　　a.

B: Not me. I _____ any soda at all since last week. I _____ water
　　　　　　　　　b.　　　　　　　　　　　　　　　　　　　　　c.

all week. It's much healthier.

3. (write)

A: Susan Jackson _____ a lot of books lately.
　　　　　　　　　　　　　a.

B: _____ she _____ *Wildest Dreams*?
　　　　　　　　　　　　　　　b.

A: Yes, she did. She _____ that one about five years ago.
　　　　　　　　　　　　　c.

4. (cook)

A: You _____ for hours. When are we eating dinner?
　　　　　a.

B: I just finished. I _____ something special for you. It's called "ants on a tree."
　　　　　　　　　　b.

A: Gross!

B: Actually, I _____ it for you many times before. It's just meatballs with rice.
　　　　　　　　c.

5. (have)

    A: I _____ a lot of trouble with my new car lately.
               _{a.}

    B: Really? You _____ it very long!
                   _{b.}

    A: I know. I _____ it for only a year. I _____ my old car for ten
                  _{c.}   _{d.}

      years before I sold it. I _____ any trouble with it at all!
                          _{e.}

6. (look)

    A: Linda _____ really discouraged yesterday afternoon.
                   _{a.}

    B: I know. She _____ for a new apartment and hasn't found anything yet.
                    _{b.}

    A: There's an apartment available on the fourth floor in our building. _____

      she _____ at it?
               _{c.}

    B: She _____ at it last week, but she didn't rent it because it's too small.
                _{d.}

VI. *Find and correct the mistake in each sentence.*

1. I ~~am~~ ^{have} applied for the position of junior accountant in my department.

2. I have been working as a bookkeeper in this company since four years.

3. I have did a good job.

4. I have already been getting a promotion.

5. I has gained a lot of experience in retail sales.

6. In addition, I have took several accounting courses.

7. Since February my boss liked my work a lot.

8. She has gave me more and more responsibility.

9. I have already show my accounting skills.

10. This has been being a very good experience for me.

▶ *To check your answers, go to the Answer Key on page 224.*

FROM GRAMMAR TO WRITING THE TOPIC SENTENCE AND PARAGRAPH UNITY

A paragraph is a group of sentences about one main idea. Writers often state the main idea in one sentence, called the topic sentence. For beginning writers, it is a good practice to put the topic sentence near the beginning of the paragraph.

 Read this personal statement for a job application. Cross out any sentences that do not belong in the paragraph.

_____

_____

While I was in high school, I worked as a server at Darby's during the summer and on weekends. ~~Summers here are very hot and humid.~~ I worked with many different kinds of customers, and I learned to be polite even with difficult people. They serve excellent food at Darby's. I received a promotion after one year. Since high school, I have been working for Steak Hut as the night manager. I have developed management skills because I supervise six employees. One of them is a good friend of mine. I have also learned to order supplies and to plan menus. Sometimes I am very tired after a night's work.

Now choose one of the sentences below as the topic sentence, and write it on the rules above the text.

- I feel that a high school education is necessary for anyone looking for a job.
- My restaurant experience has prepared me for a position with your company.
- Eating at both Darby's and Steak Hut in Greenville is very enjoyable.
- I prefer planning menus to any other task in the restaurant business.

2 *You can use a tree diagram to develop and organize your ideas.*
Complete the tree diagram for the paragraph in Exercise 1.

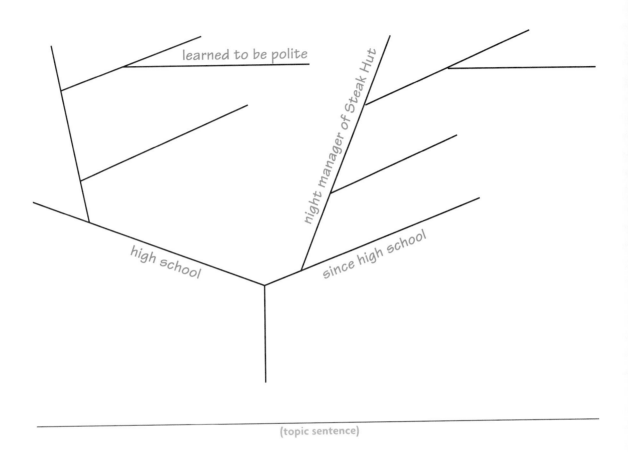

(topic sentence)

3 *Before you write . . .*

- On a separate piece of paper, make a tree diagram for your accomplishments.
  Do not include a topic sentence.

- Work with a small group. Look at each other's diagrams and develop a topic
  sentence for each one.

- Ask and answer questions to develop more information about your
  accomplishments.

4 *On a separate piece of paper, write a personal statement about your accomplishments.*
Use your tree diagram as an outline.

REVIEW OR SELFTEST
ANSWER KEY

I. (Unit 16)

2. have . . . been
3. has . . . fallen
4. 've* . . . paid
5. Have . . . written
6. hasn't read
7. 've won
8. haven't told
9. Has . . . come
10. 've had

II. (Unit 16)

2. Since, for
3. for
4. since
5. for
6. Since
7. since
8. for

III. (Units 17 and 18)

2. C
3. D
4. A
5. B
6. C
7. B
8. A
9. A
10. A

IV. (Unit 21)

2. D
3. A
4. D
5. C
6. B
7. C
8. A
9. C
10. C
11. D

V. (Units 16–21)

1. **b.** saw
2. **a.** drank OR drunk
   b. haven't drunk
   c. 've been drinking
3. **a.** has written
   b. Did . . . write
   c. wrote
4. **a.** 've been cooking
   b. cooked
   c. 've cooked
5. **a.** 've had OR 've been having
   b. haven't had
   c. 've had
   d. had
   e. didn't have
6. **a.** looked
   b. 's been looking
   c. Has . . . looked OR Did . . . look
   d. looked

VI. (Units 16–21)

2. I have been working as a
   bookkeeper in this company ~~since~~ *for*
   four years. OR since four years ago.
3. I have ~~did~~ *done* a good job.
4. I have already ~~been getting~~ *gotten* a
   promotion.
5. I ~~has~~ *have* gained a lot of experience in
   retail sales.
6. In addition, I have ~~took~~ *taken* several
   accounting courses.
7. Since February my boss ~~like~~ *has liked* my
   work a lot.
8. She has ~~gave~~ *given* me more and more
   responsibility.
9. I have already ~~show~~ *shown* my
   accounting skills.
10. This has been ~~being~~ a very good
    experience for me.

*Where a contracted form is given, the long
form is also correct.

APPENDICES

1 Irregular Verbs

BASE FORM	SIMPLE PAST	PAST PARTICIPLE
arise	arose	arisen
awake	awoke	awoken
be	was/were	been
beat	beat	beaten
become	became	become
begin	began	begun
bend	bent	bent
bet	bet	bet
bite	bit	bitten
bleed	bled	bled
blow	blew	blown
break	broke	broken
bring	brought	brought
build	built	built
burn	burned/burnt	burned/burnt
burst	burst	burst
buy	bought	bought
catch	caught	caught
choose	chose	chosen
cling	clung	clung
come	came	come
cost	cost	cost
creep	crept	crept
cut	cut	cut
deal	dealt	dealt
dig	dug	dug
dive	dived/dove	dived
do	did	done
draw	drew	drawn
dream	dreamed/dreamt	dreamed/dreamt
drink	drank	drunk
drive	drove	driven
eat	ate	eaten
fall	fell	fallen
feed	fed	fed
feel	felt	felt
fight	fought	fought
find	found	found
fit	fit	fit
flee	fled	fled
fling	flung	flung
fly	flew	flown
forbid	forbade/forbad	forbidden
forget	forgot	forgotten
forgive	forgave	forgiven
freeze	froze	frozen
get	got	gotten/got
give	gave	given
go	went	gone

BASE FORM	SIMPLE PAST	PAST PARTICIPLE
grind	ground	ground
grow	grew	grown
hang	hung	hung
have	had	had
hear	heard	heard
hide	hid	hidden
hit	hit	hit
hold	held	held
hurt	hurt	hurt
keep	kept	kept
kneel	knelt	knelt
knit	knit/knitted	knit/knitted
know	knew	known
lay	laid	laid
lead	led	led
leap	leapt	leapt
leave	left	left
lend	lent	lent
let	let	let
lie (*lie down*)	lay	lain
light	lit/lighted	lit/lighted
lose	lost	lost
make	made	made
mean	meant	meant
meet	met	met
pay	paid	paid
prove	proved	proved/proven
put	put	put
quit	quit	quit
read /rid/	read /rɛd/	read /rɛd/
ride	rode	ridden
ring	rang	rung
rise	rose	risen
run	ran	run
say	said	said
see	saw	seen
seek	sought	sought
sell	sold	sold
send	sent	sent
set	set	set
sew	sewed	sewn/sewed
shake	shook	shaken
shave	shaved	shaved/shaven
shine	shone	shone
shoot	shot	shot
show	showed	shown
shrink	shrank/shrunk	shrunk/shrunken
shut	shut	shut
sing	sang	sung

(continued on next page)

Base Form	Simple Past	Past Participle		Base Form	Simple Past	Past Participle
sink	sank	sunk		sweep	swept	swept
sit	sat	sat		swim	swam	swum
sleep	slept	slept		swing	swung	swung
slide	slid	slid		take	took	taken
speak	spoke	spoken		teach	taught	taught
speed	sped	sped		tear	tore	torn
spend	spent	spent		tell	told	told
spill	spilled/spilt	spilled/spilt		think	thought	thought
spin	spun	spun		throw	threw	thrown
spit	spit/spat	spat		understand	understood	understood
split	split	split		upset	upset	upset
spread	spread	spread		wake	woke	woken
spring	sprang	sprung		wear	wore	worn
stand	stood	stood		weave	wove	woven
steal	stole	stolen		weep	wept	wept
stick	stuck	stuck		win	won	won
sting	stung	stung		wind	wound	wound
stink	stank/stunk	stunk		withdraw	withdrew	withdrawn
strike	struck	struck		wring	wrung	wrung
swear	swore	sworn		write	wrote	written

② Common Non-action (Stative) Verbs

EMOTIONS	MENTAL STATES		WANTS AND PREFERENCES	PERCEPTION AND THE SENSES	APPEARANCE	POSSESSION
admire	agree	imagine	desire	feel	appear	belong
adore	assume	know	need	hear	be	have
appreciate	believe	mean	prefer	notice	feel	own
care	consider	presume	want	observe	look	possess
detest	disagree	realize	wish	perceive	represent	
dislike	disbelieve	recognize		see	resemble	
doubt	estimate	remember		smell	seem	
envy	expect	see (understand)		taste	signify	
fear	feel (believe)	suppose			smell	
hate	find	suspect			sound	
hope	guess	think (believe)			taste	
like	hesitate	understand				
love	hope	wonder				
regret						
respect						
trust						

③ Verbs and Expressions Commonly Used Reflexively

amuse oneself
ask oneself
avail oneself of
be hard on oneself
be oneself
be pleased with oneself
be proud of oneself
behave oneself
believe in oneself
blame oneself

cut oneself
deprive oneself of
dry oneself
enjoy oneself
feel sorry for oneself
help oneself
hurt oneself
imagine oneself
introduce oneself
kill oneself

look after oneself
look at oneself
pride oneself on
push oneself
remind oneself
see oneself
take care of oneself
talk to oneself
teach oneself
tell oneself

(s.o. = someone   s.t. = something)

PHRASAL VERB	MEANING
ask s.o. **over**	*invite to one's home*
blow s.t. **out**	*stop burning by blowing on it*
blow s.t. **up**	*make explode*
bring s.o. or s.t. **back**	*return*
bring s.o. **up**	*raise (children)*
bring s.t. **up**	*bring attention to*
burn s.t. **down**	*burn completely*
call s.o. **back**	*return a phone call*
call s.t. **off**	*cancel*
call s.o. **up**	*phone*
clean s.o. or s.t. **up**	*clean completely*
clear s.t. **up**	*clarify*
close s.t. **down**	*close by force*
cover s.o. or s.t. **up**	*cover completely*
cross s.t. **out**	*draw a line through*
do s.t. **over**	*do again*
drink s.t. **up**	*drink completely*
drop s.o. or s.t. **off**	*take someplace*
empty s.t. **out**	*empty completely*
figure s.o. or s.t. **out**	*understand (after thinking about)*
fill s.t. **in**	*complete with information*
fill s.t. **out**	*complete (a form)*
find s.t. **out**	*learn information*
give s.t. **back**	*return*
give s.t. **up**	*quit, abandon*
hand s.t. **in**	*submit work (to a boss/teacher)*
hand s.t. **out**	*distribute*
help s.o. **out**	*assist*
keep s.o. or s.t. **away**	*cause to stay at a distance*
keep s.t. **on**	*not remove (a piece of clothing/ jewelry)*
lay s.o. **off**	*end employment*
leave s.t. **on**	*not remove (a piece of clothing/ jewelry)*
leave s.t. **out**	*omit*
let s.o. **down**	*disappoint*
let s.o. **in**	*allow to enter*
let s.o. **off**	*allow to leave (a bus/car)*
light s.t. **up**	*illuminate*
look s.o. or s.t. **over**	*examine*
look s.t. **up**	*try to find (in a book/on the Internet)*
make s.t. **up**	*create*
pass s.t. **on**	*give to*
pass s.t. **out**	*distribute*
pass s.o. or s.t. **over**	*skip*

PHRASAL VERB	MEANING
pass s.o. or s.t. **up**	*decide not to use*
pay s.o. or s.t. **back**	*repay*
pick s.o. or s.t. **out**	*select*
pick s.o. or s.t. **up**	*lift*
pick s.t. **up**	*get (an idea, a new book, an interest)*
point s.o. or s.t. **out**	*indicate*
put s.t. **away**	*put in an appropriate place*
put s.t. **back**	*return to its original place*
put s.o. or s.t. **down**	*stop holding*
put s.t. **off**	*postpone*
put s.t. **on**	*cover the body*
put s.t. **together**	*assemble*
put s.t. **up**	*erect*
set s.t. **up**	1. *prepare for use*
	2. *establish (a business/an organization)*
shut s.t. **off**	*stop (a machine/light)*
start s.t. **over**	*start again*
straighten s.t. **up**	*make neat*
switch s.t. **on**	*start (a machine/light)*
take s.o. or s.t. **back**	*return*
take s.t. **off**	*remove*
talk s.o. **into**	*persuade*
talk s.t. **over**	*discuss*
tear s.t. **down**	*destroy*
tear s.t. **off**	*remove by tearing*
tear s.t. **up**	*tear into small pieces*
think s.t. **over**	*consider*
think s.t. **up**	*invent*
throw s.t. **away/out**	*discard*
try s.t. **on**	*put clothing on to see if it fits*
try s.t. **out**	*use to see if it works*
turn s.o. or s.t. **down**	*reject*
turn s.t. **down**	*lower the volume (a TV/radio)*
turn s.t. **in**	*submit*
turn s.o. or s.t. **into**	*change from one form to another*
turn s.o. **off**	*(slang) destroy interest*
turn s.t. **off**	*stop (a machine/light)*
turn s.t. **on**	*start (a machine/light)*
turn s.t. **up**	*raise the volume (a TV/radio)*
use s.t. **up**	*use completely, consume*
wake s.o. **up**	*awaken*
work s.t. **out**	*solve*
write s.t. **down**	*write on a piece of paper*
write s.t. **up**	*write in a finished form*

 Some Common Intransitive Phrasal Verbs

PHRASAL VERB	MEANING
blow up	*explode*
break down	*stop functioning*
burn down	*burn completely*
call back	*return a phone call*

PHRASAL VERB	MEANING
clear up	*become clear*
close down	*stop operating*
come about	*happen*
come along	*accompany*

PHRASAL VERB	MEANING
come in	*enter*
come off	*become unattached*
come out	*appear*
come up	*arise*

(continued on next page)   **A-3**

PHRASAL VERB	MEANING	PHRASAL VERB	MEANING	PHRASAL VERB	MEANING
dress up	*wear special clothes*	go on	*continue*	show up	*appear*
drop in	*visit unexpectedly*	grow up	*become an adult*	sign up	*register*
drop out	*quit*	hang up	*end a phone call*	sit down	*take a seat*
eat out	*eat in a restaurant*	keep away	*stay at a distance*	slip up	*make a mistake*
empty out	*empty completely*	keep on	*continue*	stand up	*rise*
find out	*learn information*	keep up	*go as fast as*	start over	*start again*
follow through	*complete*	lie down	*recline*	stay up	*remain awake*
fool around	*be playful*	light up	*illuminate*	straighten up	*make neat*
get along	*relate well*	look out	*be careful*	take off	*depart (a plane)*
get back	*return*	make up	*reconcile*	turn up	*appear*
get by	*survive*	play around	*have fun*	wake up	*arise after sleeping*
get together	*meet*	run out	*not have enough of*	watch out	*be careful*
get up	*rise from bed*	set out	*begin a project*	work out	*1. be resolved*
give up	*quit*				*2. exercise*

 ## Common Participial Adjectives

-ed	-ing	-ed	-ing	-ed	-ing
alarmed	alarming	disturbed	disturbing	moved	moving
amazed	amazing	embarrassed	embarrassing	paralyzed	paralyzing
amused	amusing	entertained	entertaining	pleased	pleasing
annoyed	annoying	excited	exciting	relaxed	relaxing
astonished	astonishing	exhausted	exhausting	satisfied	satisfying
bored	boring	fascinated	fascinating	shocked	shocking
confused	confusing	frightened	frightening	surprised	surprising
depressed	depressing	horrified	horrifying	terrified	terrifying
disappointed	disappointing	inspired	inspiring	tired	tiring
disgusted	disgusting	interested	interesting	touched	touching
distressed	distressing	irritated	irritating	troubled	troubling

 ## Irregular Comparisons of Adjectives, Adverbs, and Quantifiers

ADJECTIVE	ADVERB	COMPARATIVE	SUPERLATIVE
bad	badly	worse	worst
far	far	farther/further	farthest/furthest
good	well	better	best
little	little	less	least
many/a lot of	—	more	most
much*/a lot of	much*/a lot	more	most

*Much is usually only used in questions and negative statements.

 ## Some Adjectives that Form the Comparative and Superlative in Two Ways

ADJECTIVE	COMPARATIVE	SUPERLATIVE
common	commoner / more common	commonest / most common
cruel	crueler / more cruel	cruelest / most cruel
deadly	deadlier / more deadly	deadliest / most deadly
friendly	friendlier / more friendly	friendliest / most friendly
handsome	handsomer / more handsome	handsomest / most handsome
happy	happier / more happy	happiest / most happy
likely	likelier / more likely	likeliest / most likely
lively	livelier / more lively	liveliest / most lively
lonely	lonelier / more lonely	loneliest / most lonely
lovely	lovelier / more lovely	loveliest / most lovely
narrow	narrower / more narrow	narrowest / most narrow

ADJECTIVE	COMPARATIVE	SUPERLATIVE
pleasant	pleasanter / more pleasant	pleasantest / most pleasant
polite	politer / more polite	politest / most polite
quiet	quieter / more quiet	quietest / most quiet
shallow	shallower / more shallow	shallowest / most shallow
sincere	sincerer / more sincere	sincerest / most sincere
stupid	stupider / more stupid	stupidest / most stupid
true	truer / more true	truest / most true

9 Common Verbs Followed by the Gerund (Base Form of Verb + -ing)

acknowledge	delay	endure	give up (stop)	postpone	regret
admit	deny	enjoy	imagine	practice	report
appreciate	detest	escape	justify	prevent	resent
avoid	discontinue	explain	keep (continue)	prohibit	resist
can't help	discuss	feel like	mention	quit	risk
celebrate	dislike	finish	mind (object to)	recall	suggest
consider	dispute	forgive	miss	recommend	understand

10 Common Verbs Followed by the Infinitive (To + Base Form of Verb)

afford	can't afford	expect	learn	plan	request
agree	can't wait	fail	manage	prepare	seem
appear	choose	help	mean	pretend	want
ask	consent	hope	need	promise	wish
arrange	decide	hurry	offer	refuse	would like / 'd like
attempt	deserve	intend	pay		

11 Common Verbs Followed by the Gerund or the Infinitive

begin	forget*	love	start
can't stand	hate	prefer	stop*
continue	like	remember*	try

*These verbs can be followed by either the gerund or the infinitive, but there is a big difference in meaning (see Unit 31).

12 Verbs Followed by Objects and the Infinitive

advise	convince	help*	pay*	remind	urge
allow	encourage	hire	permit	require	want*
ask*	expect*	invite	persuade	teach	warn
cause	forbid	need*	promise*	tell	would like*
choose*	force	order			

*These verbs can also be followed by the infinitive without an object (example: ask to leave or ask someone to leave).

13 Common Adjective + Preposition Expressions

be accustomed to	be bored with/by	be fond of	be pleased about	be slow at
be afraid of	be capable of	be glad about	be ready for	be sorry for/about
be amazed at/by	be careful of	be good at	be responsible for	be surprised at/about/by
be angry at	be concerned about	be happy about	be sad about	be terrible at
be ashamed of	be content with	be interested in	be safe from	be tired of
be aware of	be curious about	be nervous about	be satisfied with	be used to
be awful at	be excited about	be opposed to	be sick of	be worried about
be bad at	be famous for			

14 Common Verb + Preposition Combinations

admit to	believe in	deal with	look forward to	resort to
advise against	choose between	dream about/of	object to	succeed in
apologize for	complain about	feel like	plan on	talk about
approve of	count on	insist on	rely on	think about

15 Spelling Rules for the Present Progressive

1. Add -*ing* to the base form of the verb.

read	read*ing*
stand	stand*ing*

2. If a verb ends in a silent -*e*, drop the final -*e* and add -*ing*.

leave	leav*ing*
take	tak*ing*

3. In a one-syllable word, if the last three letters are a consonant-vowel-consonant combination (CVC), double the last consonant before adding -*ing*.

C V C
↓ ↓ ↓
s i t   sit*ting*

C V C
↓ ↓ ↓
r u n   run*ning*

However, do not double the last consonant in words that end in *w*, *x*, or *y*.

sew	sew*ing*
fix	fix*ing*
enjoy	enjoy*ing*

4. In words of two or more syllables that end in a consonant-vowel-consonant combination, double the last consonant only if the last syllable is stressed.

admít	admit*ting*	(The last syllable is stressed)
whísper	whisper*ing*	(The last syllable is not stressed, so you don't double the -*r*.)

5. If a verb ends in -*ie*, change the *ie* to *y* before adding -*ing*.

die	d*ying*

16 Spelling Rules for the Simple Present Tense: Third-Person Singular (*he, she, it*)

1. Add -*s* for most verbs.

work	work*s*
buy	buy*s*
ride	ride*s*
return	return*s*

2. Add -*es* for words that end in -*ch*, -*s*, -*sh*, -*x*, or -*z*.

watch	watch*es*
pass	pass*es*
rush	rush*es*
relax	relax*es*
buzz	buzz*es*

3. Change the *y* to *i* and add -*es* when the base form ends in a consonant + *y*.

study	stud*ies*
hurry	hurr*ies*
dry	dr*ies*

Do not change the *y* when the base form ends in a vowel + *y*. Add -*s*.

play	play*s*
enjoy	enjoy*s*

4. A few verbs have irregular forms.

be	is
do	does
go	goes
have	has

17 Spelling Rules for the Simple Past Tense of Regular Verbs

1. If the verb ends in a consonant, add -ed.

return	return*ed*
help	help*ed*

2. If the verb ends in -e, add -d.

live	live*d*
create	create*d*
die	die*d*

3. In one-syllable words, if the verb ends in a consonant-vowel-consonant combination (CVC), double the final consonant and add -ed.

C V C
↓ ↓ ↓
h o p	hop*ped*

C V C
↓ ↓ ↓
r u b	rub*bed*

However, do not double one-syllable words ending in -w, -x, or -y.

bow	bow*ed*
mix	mix*ed*
play	play*ed*

4. In words of two or more syllables that end in a consonant-vowel-consonant combination, double the last consonant only if the last syllable is stressed.

prefér	prefer*red*	(The last syllable is stressed.)
vísit	visit*ed*	(The last syllable is not stressed, so you don't double the *t*.)

5. If the verb ends in a consonant + y, change the y to i and add -ed.

worry	worr*ied*
carry	carr*ied*

6. If the verb ends in a vowel + y, add -ed. (Do not change the y to i.)

play	play*ed*
annoy	annoy*ed*

Exceptions:

pay	paid
lay	laid
say	said

18 Spelling Rules for the Comparative (-er) and Superlative (-est) Forms of Adjectives

1. Add -er to one-syllable adjectives to form the comparative. Add -est to one-syllable adjectives to form the superlative.

cheap	cheap*er*	cheap*est*
bright	bright*er*	bright*est*

2. If the adjective ends in -e, add -r or -st.

nice	nice*r*	nice*st*

3. If the adjective ends in a consonant + y, change y to i before you add -er or -est.

pretty	prett*ier*	prett*iest*

Exception:

shy	shy*er*	shy*est*

4. If the adjective ends in a consonant-vowel-consonant combination (CVC), double the final consonant before adding -er or -est.

C V C
↓ ↓ ↓
b i g	big*ger*	big*gest*

However, do not double the consonant in words ending in -w or -y.

slow	slow*er*	slow*est*
coy	coy*er*	coy*est*

19 Spelling Rules for Adverbs Ending in -ly

1. Add -ly to the corresponding adjective.

nice	nice*ly*
quiet	quiet*ly*
beautiful	beautiful*ly*

2. If the adjective ends in a consonant + y, change the y to i before adding -ly.

easy	eas*ily*

3. If the adjective ends in -le, drop the e and add -y.

possible	possib*ly*

However, do not drop the e for other adjectives ending in -e.

extreme	extreme*ly*

Exception:

true	tru*ly*

4. If the adjective ends in -ic, add -ally.

basic	basic*ally*
fantastic	fantastic*ally*

1. SIMPLE PRESENT TENSE, PRESENT PROGRESSIVE, AND IMPERATIVE

Contractions with *Be*

I am	=	**I'm**
you are	=	**you're**
he is	=	**he's**
she is	=	**she's**
it is	=	**it's**
we are	=	**we're**
you are	=	**you're**
they are	=	**they're**

SIMPLE PRESENT	**PRESENT PROGRESSIVE**
I**'m** a student.	I**'m studying** here.
He**'s** my teacher.	He**'s teaching** verbs.
We**'re** from Canada.	We**'re living** here.

I am not	=	**I'm not**		
you are not	=	**you're not**	or	**you aren't**
he is not	=	**he's not**	or	**he isn't**
she is not	=	**she's not**	or	**she isn't**
it is not	=	**it's not**	or	**it isn't**
we are not	=	**we're not**	or	**we aren't**
you are not	=	**you're not**	or	**you aren't**
they are not	=	**they're not**	or	**they aren't**

SIMPLE PRESENT	**PRESENT PROGRESSIVE**
She**'s not** sick.	She**'s not reading.**
He **isn't** late.	He **isn't coming.**
We **aren't** twins.	We **aren't leaving.**
They**'re not** here.	They**'re not playing.**

Contractions with *Do*

do not	=	**don't**
does not	=	**doesn't**

SIMPLE PRESENT	**IMPERATIVE**
They **don't live** here.	**Don't run**!
It **doesn't snow** much.	

2. SIMPLE PAST TENSE AND PAST PROGRESSIVE

Contractions with *Be*

was not	=	**wasn't**
were not	=	**weren't**

SIMPLE PAST	**PAST PROGRESSIVE**
He **wasn't** a poet.	He **wasn't singing.**
They **weren't** twins.	They **weren't sleeping**.
We **didn't** see her.	

Contractions with *Do*

did not	=	**didn't**

3. FUTURE

Contractions with *Will*

I will	=	**I'll**
you will	=	**you'll**
he will	=	**he'll**
she will	=	**she'll**
it will	=	**it'll**
we will	=	**we'll**
you will	=	**you'll**
they will	=	**they'll**

will not	=	**won't**

FUTURE WITH *WILL*
I**'ll take** the train.
It**'ll be** faster that way.
We**'ll go** together.
He **won't come** with us.
They **won't miss** the train.

Contractions with *Be going to*

I am going to	=	**I'm going to**
you are going to	=	**you're going to**
he is going to	=	**he's going to**
she is going to	=	**she's going to**
it is going to	=	**it's going to**
we are going to	=	**we're going to**
you are going to	=	**you're going to**
they are going to	=	**they're going to**

FUTURE WITH *BE GOING TO*
I**'m going to buy** tickets tomorrow.
She**'s going to call** you.
It**'s going to rain** soon.
We**'re going to drive** to Boston.
They**'re going to crash**!

4. PRESENT PERFECT AND PRESENT PERFECT PROGRESSIVE

Contractions with *Have*

I have	=	**I've**
you have	=	**you've**
he has	=	**he's**
she has	=	**she's**
it has	=	**it's**
we have	=	**we've**
you have	=	**you've**
they have	=	**they've**
have not	=	**haven't**
has not	=	**hasn't**

You**'ve** already **read** that page.
We**'ve been writing** for an hour.
She**'s been** to Africa three times.
It**'s been raining** since yesterday.
We **haven't seen** any elephants yet.
They **haven't been living** here long.

5. MODALS AND MODAL-LIKE EXPRESSIONS

cannot or can not	=	**can't**
could not	=	**couldn't**
should not	=	**shouldn't**
had better	=	**'d better**
would prefer	=	**'d prefer**
would not	=	**wouldn't**
would rather	=	**'d rather**

She **can't dance**.
We **shouldn't go**.
They**'d better decide**.
I**'d prefer** coffee.
She **wouldn't**.
I**'d rather take** the bus.

21 Pronunciation Table

These are the pronunciation symbols used in this text. Listen to the pronunciation of the key words.

VOWELS

Symbol	Key Word
i	beat, feed
ɪ	bit, did
eɪ	date, paid
ɛ	bet, bed
æ	bat, bad
ɑ	box, odd, father
ɔ	bought, dog
oʊ	boat, road
ʊ	book, good
u	boot, food, student
ʌ	but, mud, mother
ə	banana, among
ɚ	shirt, murder
aɪ	bite, cry, buy, eye
aʊ	about, how
ɔɪ	voice, boy
ɪr	beer
ɛr	bare
ɑr	bar
ɔr	door
ʊr	tour

CONSONANTS

Symbol	Key Word	Symbol	Key Word
p	pack, happy	ʃ	ship, machine, station, special, discussion
b	back, rubber	ʒ	measure, vision
t	tie	h	hot, who
d	die	m	men
k	came, key, quick	n	sun, know, pneumonia
g	game, guest	ŋ	sung, ringing
tʃ	church, nature, watch	w	wet, white
dʒ	judge, general, major	l	light, long
f	fan, photograph	r	right, wrong
v	van	y	yes, use, music
θ	thing, breath	ţ	butter, bottle
ð	then, breathe		
s	sip, city, psychology		
z	zip, please, goes		

STRESS
' shows main stress.

22 Pronunciation Rules for the Simple Present Tense: Third-Person Singular *(he, she, it)*

1. The third-person singular in the simple present tense always ends in the letter -s. There are, however, three different pronunciations for the final sound of the third person singular.

/s/	/z/	/ɪz/
talks	loves	dances

2. The final sound is pronounced /s/ after the voiceless sounds /p/, /t/, /k/, and /f/.

top	tops
get	gets
take	takes
laugh	laughs

3. The final sound is pronounced /z/ after the voiced sounds /b/, /d/, /g/, /v/, /ð/, /m/, /n/, /ŋ/, /l/, and /r/.

describe	describes
spend	spends
hug	hugs
live	lives
bathe	bathes
seem	seems
remain	remains
sing	sings
tell	tells
lower	lowers

4. The final sound is pronounced /z/ after all vowel sounds.

agree	agrees
try	tries
stay	stays
know	knows

5. The final sound is pronounced /ɪz/ after the sounds /s/, /z/, /ʃ/, /ʒ/, /tʃ/, and /dʒ/. /ɪz/ adds a syllable to the verb.

relax	relaxes
freeze	freezes
rush	rushes
massage	massages
watch	watches
judge	judges

6. *Do* and *say* have a change in vowel sound.

say	/seɪ/	says	/sɛz/
do	/du/	does	/dʌz/

23 Pronunciation Rules for the Simple Past Tense of Regular Verbs

1. The regular simple past always ends in the letter -d. There are, however, three different pronunciations for the final sound of the regular simple past.

/t/	/d/	/ɪd/
raced	lived	attended

2. The final sound is pronounced /t/ after the voiceless sounds /p/, /k/, /f/, /s/, /ʃ/, and /tʃ/.

hop	hopped
work	worked
laugh	laughed
address	addressed
publish	published
watch	watched

3. The final sound is pronounced /d/ after the voiced sounds /b/, /g/, /v/, /z/, /ʒ/, /dʒ/, /m/, /n/, /ŋ/, /l/, /r/, and /ð/.

rub	rubbed	rhyme	rhymed
hug	hugged	return	returned
live	lived	bang	banged
surprise	surprised	enroll	enrolled
massage	massaged	appear	appeared
change	changed	bathe	bathed

4. The final sound is pronounced /d/ after all vowel sounds.

agree	agreed
play	played
die	died
enjoy	enjoyed

5. The final sound is pronounced /ɪd/ after /t/ and /d/. /ɪd/ adds a syllable to the verb.

start	started
decide	decided

INDEX

This Index is for the full and split editions. All entries are in the full book.
Entries for Volume A of the split edition are in black. Entries for Volume B are in color.